ADDICTED

Our Strength Under the Influence

ANNIE AUGUSTUS ROSE

Acclaim for Annie Augustus Rose's

ADDICTED
Our Strength Under the Influence

Kudos to Annie for undertaking the heartbreaking task of sharing her family's story in such a unique and meaningful way. It is truly a gift to the world. Much of it is in real time as Annie shares emails and letters. Incredibly powerful. Annie brings the reader into the lives of her family as they painfully learn and grow each step of the way, getting up and dusting themselves off to go forward even when things don't go as planned on this perilous and, too often, never-ending journey. It reveals the raw emotion, the elation, the deep disappointment, the despair. It is not about the difference between right and wrong but rather about options, describing how strategies worked, and giving the reader the opportunity to decide for themselves the path they want to take. It shows, in glaring detail, the ways "the system" has failed, and continues to fail so many vulnerable people. A must read for anyone who cares about people who are addicted or who are addicted themselves. These days that is everyone — family members, friends, co-workers, neighbors, community members, young and old, all ethnicities and sexual orientations, rich or poor, people everywhere.

Mary Ellen Copeland, Ph.D
Mental health recovery author, educator and advocate

What a tumultuous ride this family has been on! The letters were certainly eye-opening, detailing the struggle and the war a daughter, mother and father were in. The individual writings of the grandkids were really eye-opening too, as to the long reaching trauma that ensued from a parent's addiction. This memoir serves as a valuable archive that records the everyday life of several generations in the throes of drug addiction and mental health issues.

Kathleen Maisto
Retired academic, career counselor and transfer coordinator
Greenfield Community College

Reading this book was an emotional experience. I felt like I was falling through a dark tunnel, once in a while being able to grab on to some support on the way down, but always losing my grip and continuing the fall; never reaching a destination, just continuing the fall. Annie describes the horror that a family goes through when confronted with addiction in a very matter of fact and understandable way. The pain felt by all is very real. It is clear that our society is not approaching addiction in the right way.

Joanne Corey
Retired middle school science teacher

Annie Augustus Rose has written a raw and compelling memoir, giving the reader a front-row seat into the devastating effects addiction has on several generations of a family. The story of addiction goes far beyond the addict. The reader can feel the heavy weight of sadness, anxiety, disappointment, desperation, and anger, which is always mixed with hope. The author displays great courage in making the difficult decision to raise her grandchildren, giving them stability, all while dealing with the unimaginable stresses of the unpredictability of the addict. This book will certainly offer a lifeline to any family member dealing with a loved one's addiction. This book is also a must-read for people who have never experienced the effects of addiction, as it breaks the stigma that the addicts and their families live with every day. Law enforcement and health care professionals would also benefit from the book, as it can open doors to better, more compassionate treatment for addicts. The book also highlights the story of the author's own growth and transformation. She shows grace, courage, resilience, intelligence, and love, as she creates the local Nar-Anon group that has helped so many others in similar circumstances.

Robin Matathias
Adjunct professor
Keene State College

ADDICTED

Our Strength Under the Influence

ANNIE AUGUSTUS ROSE

CCE PUBLISHING
Edgewater, Florida

This book is a work of nonfiction.
Certain places, names of people and identifying characteristics
have been changed.

My memory is imperfect, but in this memoir
I'm sharing to the best of my knowledge
how I have remembered certain events.

Cover image: Used under license from Luka/Adobe Stock
Family tree image: Janet Hovorka/Family ChartMasters
Cover and book design: Cindy Casey/CCE Publishing

Published by
CCE PUBLISHING
Edgewater, Florida
ccepublishing.com
cindycaseyediting@gmail.com

Printed in the United States of America

Paperback ISBN: 979-8-987-3464-0-2
Hardback ISBN: 979-8-987-3464-1-9

Dedication

For Mom, my life-giver.
Foremost my friend and mentor, my rock, always my cheerleader.
I am of you, failure is not an option.
Miss your face, your smile, your hugs.

ADDICTED: Our Strength Under the Influence

Table of Contents

The Family Defined

Bumpa: maternal grandfather

Nana: maternal grandmother

Gordon: father

Sarah: mother

Annie: author

Jerry: former husband and father to Greg and Jamie

Greg: son of Jerry and Annie

Lyn: former wife of Greg, mother to Andrew and Cassie

Andrew: Greg and Lyn's son

Cassie: Greg and Lyn's daughter

Jamie: daughter of Jerry and Annie

Eric: former husband of Jamie, father to Camille and Josh

Camille: daughter of Jamie and Eric

Molly: daughter of Camille

Josh: son of Jamie and Eric

Emily: daughter of Jamie and Luis

Chris: my partner of 15 years

Rosemary: my childhood best friend, mother of Mike

Mike: son of Rosemary, boyfriend of Jamie, person who introduced her to heroin

Matty: young man Jamie met at rehab, also heroin addicted, second husband

Kelly: girlfriend of Jamie

Luis: father of Emily

Joan: my sister

April: friend of Jamie, my foster-daughter

Judy: second and third wife to Jerry

Prologue

Get ready for a bumpy ride. There is nothing smooth, easy, or comfortable ahead. Fragmented, heartbreaking, devastating, and soul-crushing? Yes, you'll find all these emotions to be true, for this is the path of a family crashing head on into the life-altering reality of addiction.

My daughter Jamie, after more than two decades of heroin addiction, has been in and out of the process of recovery multiple times. On a separate, but parallel trajectory, my son Gregory has found himself unable to escape the clutches of long-term addiction to crack cocaine and then heroin, too. The generational damage left behind is undeniable and far-reaching.

Much comfort is derived from the familiarity of home.

We are of our family roots.

Those thoughts emerged as I began to imagine the idea of sharing my family's story. Through my lived experiences over these many years, I developed a passion for the obvious, to help my grandchildren toward a path of success by offering a guiding hand with love and stability. This was not always easy and I wasn't always successful in my approach. Yet, I was committed to staying the course as each challenge presented itself.

Now that you have been drawn to this book, as you read along you may even see yourself here. Helping you, the reader, is simply the goal of this memoir.

When my husband and I decided to start a family, we could not have imagined what was to become this reality. Within these pages, as you will find, when faced with the adversity of these challenging and often heartbreaking years, commitment was the basis for staring it down and sometimes holding on for dear life.

One day, about twenty or so years ago, when asked on a Casey Family (more about that inside) questionnaire, "How have you changed as you've grown older?"

I replied, "I continued to be adventuresome. I love to travel. I remain strong-willed, and I believe these are all a part of my personality – who I am.

"As I see it, these traits and others have carried me in good times and in bad. If I were not adventuresome, I certainly would not have been able to face the many challenges presented to me... and now, having embarked on this new path of raising my grandchildren.

"Strong-willed, stubborn, focused, these facets of who I am allow me to complete the task at hand, to stay the course, so to speak."

Each experience in my life – be it childbirth, raising children, divorce, earning a successful living as a single parent that allowed me to provide for my family, physical illness, remarriage, subsequent divorce, dating, grief at loss – have all contributed to the person I am today.

Through all of this I found my voice, self-confidence. Married at a time (1965) when women were viewed as the "Mrs." – always second in line to the man of the house. I believed, too, that we were convinced through the marketing of shows like "Leave It to Beaver" that life was simply grand without any pitfalls.

Of course, anyone who has been married knows this is a myth.

Next question: "Are there ways you would like to change your life over the next few years?" (And wasn't that a loaded question?)

To which I replied, "Through my most recent experience with my own family, I have developed a passion to help my grandchildren toward a path of success in their lives. Now that I have additional first-hand information (there's that recurring phrase, "lived experience") I only wish to apply it to the challenges that lay ahead of me.

"It would be of interest to help others who have found themselves in similar familial situations. Much information has come my way in the past two years and I am hopeful that one day I can achieve this goal. I know this will happen in time."

One could say I believe in me. Something from deep inside, an unbridled desire has convinced me over and over again to hold my head high in each day and yet at the same time, keep my eyes focused toward tomorrow.

Isn't this all about the art of living with intention, making a difference that will impact the life of a child in ways yet to be defined?

At age 40, I was diagnosed with ovarian cancer. I am now 75. I survived ovarian cancer and I have survived this, too.

I didn't give up easily – I just didn't give up. For me, this crisis presented an opportunity for a second chance at parenting, learning new skills, understanding the importance of setting limits and boundaries, and correcting certain family patterns to significantly change the course of all our lives.

Under the weight of addiction, my family continues to survive this unsteady and often unpredictable course because, together, we are rooted in strength.

Much as we go through our own life cycles, the tree, like my family, cycles and survives. Green buds that arrive in springtime bring forth foliage; nourished by gentle rain, leaves burst forth into their brilliant display of colors. Between the branches and under the boughs, a tree offers protected shelter. Then, with winter's frost, it offers a time to rest and renew, quiet, only to emerge once again.

Secure in its roots, the tree nurtures. Under the weight of addiction, we continue to endure because, together, we are rooted in strength.

Be forewarned that the narrative of this book is uncomfortable; words will mirror the brutal emotional roller coaster our family members have been forced to ride for decades. Maybe you can identify with these patterns. Buckle up.

~ *Chapter 1* ~

The Dragon

The tail of the heroin dragon is uncontrollable. Visualize a gnarled, spiked weapon, swiftly and viciously impaling the vulnerable and afflicted while taking down families in its path of destruction. This is the true nature of addiction – and how this powerful "brain disease" can turn a once beautiful, intelligent, viable child into prey.

There is also the tongue of the dragon – its humanized voice. Have you heard it coming through an addicted friend or loved one? The dragon is relentless in its pursuit, and seeks to convince everyone of the venomous words and promises it spews.

When talking with a person with substance use disorder (SUD), you might imagine "good angel, bad devil" to understand the grip of this nasty, foul dragon. Picture them sitting high atop the shoulders of your friend or loved one. The good angel, who imagines an experience of recovery (if only for a short moment in time), will remark, "Yes, recovery! This is THE path, one I will follow to help rebuild and save my life. I just need to keep my eye on the prize."

Imagine, too, the long-term devil of addiction sitting on the other shoulder, his spiky tail swishing impatiently as he waits for his next victim, ready to pounce and override any thought of recovery. In mere seconds, all hopes are dashed. Recovery might come someday, but not today. The devil wins again.

Without development of a better understanding of addiction as a brain disease, nothing will change. In the broader sense, this will require far more than a generalized understanding of addiction. We need to understand stigma in the context of the attitudes of the people on the front lines: in hospital emergency rooms, in law enforcement, in the judicial system. I write with firsthand knowledge that people who suffer from addiction are characteristically treated inhumanely. Many can attest to this tragedy of the human experience. The life of the addict can be compared to a New England dirt road during any given mud season: unpredictable, a quagmire lying in wait to swallow up anyone attempting to pass.

Yes, there is plenty of help emerging today; yet if the addicted person doesn't want that help, how do you get them to change their thinking? Therein lies the rub – even with all the understanding a community can muster.

~ *Chapter 2* ~

A Word About Commitment

Since those days when I learned about the addictions facing down each of my children, my commitment has endured as a formal promise and declaration of assurance to myself, my children and family members, and, ultimately, to our community. Like myself, perhaps necessity brought you to this place, but now your heart is involved.

A word of caution

ALL IN. You will need to be "all in" because without this commitment, success will elude your good intentions.

Be prepared. You will be exhausted, angry at times, and ready to take a one-way ride to anywhere but here. Taking care of yourself however you can, by any healthy means doesn't always come easy, but if you have to get up earlier in your day than usual, take a walk around your neighborhood and get yourself ready to face the day.

My biggest ally has been knowledge through education. This has been the key to my survival – not to mention support from my partner and close personal friends, psychotherapy, our monthly home team meetings, consistent and rigorous physical exercise, meditation, respite, and my local NarAnon Support Group.

Believe in yourself. This is all about the art of living with intention, making a difference in one or a thousand small ways that will forever impact the physical, psychological, emotional and spiritual health of your family.

I am an ovarian cancer survivor. You could say I don't give up easily. In the end, the almost indescribable crisis of my daughter's addiction created an opportunity: a second chance at parenting, learning new skills, setting limitations and boundaries to understand and correct our family pattern while significantly changing the course of all our lives.

Through the course of many years as an executive assistant in the workplace, little did I know that I was, in fact, training for the bigger picture. How could I have known this experience would define my purpose here on Earth?

~ Chapter 3 ~

Raising Grandchildren:
How it all began

Recent medical findings describe addiction as a chronic brain disease. Yet while this remains a controversial concept many find challenging, what I can confirm to you is this: addiction is a family disease. How could the single action of one individual affect the lives of so many – forever? Acceptance of addiction as a diagnosable disease is still a controversial concept that many find challenging.

In my experience, addiction (to whatever it may be: alcohol, food, heroin, gambling, sex, even shopping) is a disease that a person simply does not knowingly invite into their lives. I am quite certain that any individual with alcohol or drug dependency will tell you they did not wake up one morning and say, "Today, I will become an addict." That person did not comprehend that by "picking up" a drink, pill or fix, their lives would be changed forever. It happened by his or her hand, but not as a result of clear or focused intention. This is the insidious nature of addiction.

If you will, go back with me and listen. Addiction is no stranger to my family. My maternal grandfather, "Bumpa," as he was known to me, was a proud World War I veteran – hardworking, fun-loving, and devoted to his family. Yet in so many ways, everyone in the family held a secret. Bumpa was chronically addicted to alcohol, and his excessive drinking was often unbearable to his family. The lives of my grandmother, my mother and her two siblings were altered along the way by embarrassment, isolating shame and silence all because no one talked about the fact that Bumpa had a drinking problem. They were all held hostage at home behind closed doors unable to have friends visit or plan ahead for family meals or celebrations due to the unpredictable nature of their home life. As a result, I witnessed my mother's adult life forever impacted as a result of his actions; indeed, she described it as "hell on earth."

How could the single action of one individual affect the lives of so many? It has the power to do this because addiction is a family disease.

I remember the moment with great clarity: the ordinary Sunday afternoon in September 1998 when my daughter told me she was addicted to heroin. My own life was cruelly changed in an instant, and ever since then, every aspect of it has been influenced by drug addiction. At the time, I had no inkling of the extent to which it would affect not only me, but every single member of my family – most tragically of all, my grandchildren, the children of my addicted children. I would soon discover how my daughter's actions would directly and permanently affect and change our entire family. I was about to accept the biggest challenge of my life.

Borne of chaos, opportunity knocks. Your heart opens to the possibilities. You could say I was spurred to action. To my daughter's credit, a detox bed at a nearby drug rehabilitation facility had been secured earlier that Sunday, and before I knew it, we were in the car, driving, driving, driving. Already exhausted from the weekend, my mind was a blur, my thoughts a jumble. What was my next move going to be? Reaching our destination and after leaving Jamie in good care, I drove back toward home, recalling the words "*one day at a time,*" and reciting the words to the Serenity Prayer over and over, "*God grant me the serenity to accept the things I cannot change, courage to change the things I can, and the wisdom to know the difference.*"

As I drove along, what followed was eerie calm, then a

feeling, I am not alone.

At this parallel in my life, I had just entered into a new relationship, one in which I felt deep love for and connection with my partner, Chris.

Having been friends for several years, Chris and I were committed to one another in a loving, caring and respectful relationship. We were actually both taken quite by surprise at the ease at which our romantic feelings developed. Founded in friendship and trust, we had openness in our ability to communicate with one another that was the basis for who we were as a couple.

I had the greatest respect and admiration for Chris and knew as soon as we started dating that I wanted to spend the rest of my life with her.

So now what was to become of that? How would this deeply personal turn of events impact our possibility at building a life together?

God listens, "I am not alone." God is with me. Simple words, yet are all encompassing. We had no way to know what was in store for our journey together, yet I believed Chris entered my life at one of those crossroads, our decision to partner would prove merit time and time again as we entered into the realm of the future.

What was to come was not the existence we had imagined and certainly never discussed, yet there was something very special about "us" together.

Chris in her mid-40s, with no biological children of her own, would often repeat, "I came from a life that was predictable, even boring; black and white, there was no gray. My life now, gray occasionally, words defy imagination mostly."

I was drawn to Chris' sense of humor right from "hello." I admired the way she looked on the bright side always with a positive attitude – a characteristic that would soon be put to the test. It was, however, her fun-loving, yet genuine self that she forged strong personal bonds with Camille and Josh and it was no surprise how she was able to easily integrate herself into the oft fragile nature their lives had become, developing trust with each passing day.

Early on in their relationship, Camille remarked that if it had not been for Chris, she and her grandmother would have "done each other in." As Camille and Chris spent more time together, a true friendship developed while her role of referee had its place to keep the peace, it was that of mentor that made an indelible difference in Camille's young life.

With no surprise, sports, particularly football and the New England Patriots, brought a common interest between Chris and Josh. Tedy Bruschi became a household name. During the season, you could feel the excitement in the air as they wore their number 54 game-day shirts to cheer on their team from our living room.

As you have already read, we were embedded in chaos. We – Chris and I – morphed into a household of four with the unexpected addition of Camille and Josh. Yet, the nature of addiction is never predictable and as you will soon learn, eventually with the addition of toddler Emily at age 3, we became a family of five. Chris was very resistant, but our situation simply did not offer options for me. It became a time of strife between us, the idea of adding one more child was overwhelming. Yet, with time and weekend visitation with Emily in our home, Chris came to a place of acceptance and as the bond between them grew stronger, she opened her heart with love.

In my mind's eye, even today as I sit and reflect on the past, it is Halloween. Chris and Emily are sitting on the floor of her bedroom and with wild imagination, scissors and tape in hands have artfully created costumes for her menagerie of stuffed animals that surround them. Is there no greater way to love a child than to spend time together?

In addition to managing evolving family responsibilities for our now expanded family, Chris and I held demanding and often exhausting full time jobs. Regardless of this unexpected twist, not only was employment a large part of our financial support system, long ago, each of us with a strong work ethic, were personally committed to "show up" to the best of our ability every day. At first, our employers were understanding. However, as time dragged along, and with their businesses to maintain, the direct impact of our occasional unreliability was troubling.

Suddenly, my child was in rehab. With my usual sense of optimism rebounding, I became convinced that we were only living in temporary insanity. Once the rehab program was completed, I thought, my grandchildren would return to their mother, and our lives would return to their usual rhythm. Sanity would be restored.

No.

What I didn't realize was this: that September day represented the beginning of the end of my child's ability to function as a full-time parent.

When my grandchildren first came to live with us in 1998, I was unknowingly unrealistic in my expectations. Camille and Joshua were my grandchildren. How hard could this be? I had been a parent before, and we would just go about the business of living our lives until my daughter got better, right?

Was I mistaken to apply logical thinking to the situation? Absolutely.

After many attempts at rehabilitation, I realized with sadness that my daughter was not getting better. In fact, her life seemed to be spiraling downward – the disease of substance use. I realized we would have to dig in and make the best of the situation. And only then did I begin to understand the chaotic nature of the existence my grandchildren had been enduring for many years.

The daily scramble began to rearrange our world. Initially, because I was living in a different township from my grandchildren, long rides to and from school, challenging logistical puzzles, and endless coordination of schedule changes were required of us all. The upheaval for my grandchildren was extreme. They did not want to be living with me, or us; they wanted to be in their own familiar surroundings, and they let me know in so many, many ways.

In the meantime, with her first rehab not even completed, my daughter made a run for it with another inpatient, and together, they left the facility. Jamie ended up marrying her acquaintance…a man 10 years her junior. She had known him less than a month. A short while later, another failed attempt at rehab; this time, both marriage counseling and another round of drug treatment walked hand-in-hand for my child.

My grandchildren were ages seven and nine, and I was fifty-two when they came to stay that day in September. Very suddenly, my partner Chris became a first-time parent. For nine months in 1998, my grandchildren lived with us, and during that time, the many facets of their behavior revealed themselves. Were my eyes ever opened!

As time passed, the ripple effect of addiction continued to take a heavy toll on us all.

Despite the unwelcomed impact, Chris and I were an unstoppable team, determined as we nurtured our new family in the best possible ways. We were, however, blindly unrealistic in our expectations. How hard could this be?

We loved each other, always careful to try and plan time together whenever possible. We were filled with the promise of a "can-do" spirit, a very natural part of who we were individually.

Camille and Josh were very energetic, requiring our attention, as much as we could give. Camille was especially hypersensitive to noise and had great difficulty relaxing under any circumstance while Josh was full of rage and anger, ready to explode when things didn't go his way. We quickly realized though as we watched each child act out in their own emotional way, we needed to consult professional advice and turned to their pediatrician for guidance. Given their early exposure to trauma in their family home, there was no question Camille and Josh needed support and soon thereafter they began to meet regularly with their own psychotherapists.

Both grandchildren were eventually diagnosed with attention deficit disorder, along with myriad psychological diagnoses: PTSD, depression and anger (all of which led to behavioral difficulties at school), low self-esteem, antisocial behavior, hypervigilance with resultant sleep deprivation.

Chris and I could barely keep up with the ever-changing daily landscape ... but we did. In retrospect, I believe our success standing ground was due in part to the stability she experienced at a young age from her birth family. This was a strength Chris contributed time and again to this family throughout our time together. Introduced to Individual Education (504) Plans, we were grateful for these academic supports that would help my grandchildren cope at school and at home, too.

We were learning as fast as we could, absorbing the new world around us. It became apparent during this period that regardless of the addiction, my grandchildren still needed a connection with their birth parents. From time to time, I allowed my daughter to visit with Camille and Joshua at our home. Looking back, I know I was rationalizing these visits, because we were suffering ourselves, and JUST NEEDED A BREAK! Frankly, we were exhausted: working full time, driving and parenting without a break in the action, 24 hours a day, seven days a week.

Eric and Jamie met in high school. Several years older, he joined the Army right after graduation. Camille was born while Jamie was in twelfth grade. She graduated as planned and later that summer, they married, remaining together long enough for her to become pregnant with Josh. Chaos and immaturity ensued and before that new baby was born, they separated.

There was a divorce and for years following, Jamie intentionally kept Camille and Josh from seeing their biological dad, Eric, and oddly enough, he seemed okay with that arrangement.

Now, though, under these circumstances in our lives, with what felt like a desperate stretch, I called him on the phone. However, this was not the first time in recent months. When Camille and Josh came to live with us, it was not a legal arrangement but simply us caring for my grandchildren who could no longer safely live with their mother.

On the attempt to enroll them in our school district, I learned I would need to become a court-appointed guardian for both children and part of that application process required signed permission from each biological parent. It was only during that first phone call to Eric when he became aware of the serious nature of Jamie's addiction and how it was affecting their children. He did not contest my request of the court.

So now I wanted him to become a part of their lives after a void of many years. Surprisingly, he was amenable; they were a part of him after all. We made an agreement for visitation, us mostly with the hope it would benefit all, but especially for Camille and Josh to re-establish a relationship with their dad.

Eventually, Jamie left her new husband and came back to our town to live. She was constantly disruptive, calling, stopping by and bringing the chaos of addiction into our home. When she refused to allow me to be fully responsible for the children, I demanded, exasperated, that she take Camille and Josh back. Upon that request in March 1999, they left our home for almost a year.

Although I felt some relief, I was devastated, concerned for my grandchildren and the days that lay ahead for them.

Chris and I tried to pick up the pieces. During this "putting our lives back together" scenario, we both enrolled in the local NAMI Family to Family 12 week education course. It was a preparedness step in part for us to gain a better understanding of what we had been through and what surely would be coming around again.

My daughter's behavior did not immediately improve. In fact, she continued to make poor decisions. We tried to remain optimistic, encouraging her in every way possible to get the help she needed so she could eventually turn her life around.

The children's lives were in chaos, and ours, too, even though they were not living with us. During this time, I retained guardianship. But when I received a disturbing telephone call from the school principal on the snowy morning of February 17, 2000, I *knew* the familiar patterns of Jamie's drug use once more had control of her life. I went to the school and brought them home with me and it was then that I realized, my grandchildren would most likely never live in their family home again.

The biggest boost to my own recovery also came in the year 2000 when I learned about NarAnon Family Groups. A companion program to Narcotics Anonymous, NarAnon was founded in the late 1960s in California, and had 12-step chapters worldwide, but none yet within realistic traveling distance from where I lived. I thought "why not?" bring a chapter to my hometown, I couldn't be the only person or parent who could benefit from this type of support. Like anything new, it took time for people to find this meeting; yet with perseverance, we were eventually launched and now years later, this is the same weekly meeting I continue to facilitate today.

As I often remind this NarAnon audience, drug dependency, like many other addictions, is considered a family disease, and family members should be encouraged to attend meetings as soon as a drug issue is suspected.

NarAnon offers a constructive program that allows members to achieve peace of mind and hope. They learn to accept addiction as a disease. As a result, a better understanding ensues which can help reduce family tension, and offer encouragement to the substance user to seek help.

During this period, an added complication arose; my employer of twenty years made a decision to sell his company to a competing business. Initially, I was told my job was secure, but not long afterward, my position was eliminated, and I found myself seeking unemployment benefits. To say that things happen for all the right reasons, one has to trust, but in my case, I believe my higher power was working overtime.

I received a company "retirement package" that would see me through until I could find further employment, which was exactly what I intended to do. Collecting unemployment gave me a bit of a cushion, and despite Chris's financial contribution from her fulltime job, it was undeniable we would need substantial funds to support our now growing family.

I actively sought out employment, but when I was invited for a third interview, reality took hold. The difficulties at school, particularly for my grandson, were so great that I knew it would be unrealistic for me to even consider being 45 minutes out of reach in another state. Sadly, I declined the interview – and, as a result, my unemployment benefits were abruptly terminated. However, I quickly learned that I could appeal the decision, and made an appointment to challenge the state's ruling. Again, an intervention of faith: the judge, siding with my rationale, ruled in my favor. My past benefits were reimbursed, and unemployment benefits were reinstated. God was truly holding my hand.

And in the order of all things good, I learned about a private foster care foundation called Casey Family Services, and quickly made a connection with them.

In the beginning, I knew little other than their name but

also understood the potential of what their presence could mean in our lives.

Founded in 1966, the mission of the Casey Family programs were focused primarily on helping kinship or foster families provide a safe environment in which to raise children who could not live with their biological parents.

Our family qualified, and after a lengthy application process, we were accepted under their umbrella. Once established, my financial concerns were extinguished. I ceased having to think about finding a job; I could be a real stay-at-home parent. And I was.

Support services were provided, including individual and family therapy, room-and-board stipends, clothing, summer camp, and yes, even a washer and dryer for our home. No reasonable request was denied.

When I think of that time period, tireless advocacy comes to mind. I continued to navigate my way through peaks and valleys. In addition to Casey resources, organizations such as HCRS (Health Care and Rehabilitation Services) and, NAMI (National Alliance on Mental Illness) were invaluable resources to guide us.

I spent time reading and acquainted myself with various authors whose expertise on the subject of addiction, guided me toward answers to an ever-evolving set of questions. Attending professional seminars and conferences piqued my interest, and I learned something new from each one.

Out of necessity we developed monthly home team meetings. Anyone including individual psychotherapists, teachers, school counselors, any person working with our family was welcome at the table where we shared ideas and collaborated together.

This pivotal idea proved to be vital and once our group was established, Chris and I felt support and validation as we made decisions on behalf of our family. And I would like to add, should you find yourself in a similar situation to ours, don't hesitate to surround yourself with people who care about your family.

Did I mention the weekly grandparents' support group? This was an awesome sounding board that along with two professional psychotherapists helped me maintain my balance and allowed me to make a new set of friends, people whose circumstances were like mine; we were unified by a common theme.

In 2001, Jamie gave birth to a third child, Emily, who was born to her heroin dependent mother. The first 30 days of this child's life were spent in withdrawal from prenatal exposure to opioids in the neonatal unit of a nearby hospital. Due to the circumstances surrounding her birth, her discharge was approved only if a prearranged safe place could be found. Jerry and his wife, Judy, offered Jamie and Emily a home with them until arrangements could be made for them to live in a group home for mothers in recovery.

Eventually, Emily came to live with us, and at the age of three, I adopted her into permanence ... but I am getting ahead of myself here.

In 2007, as a form of self-care, I purchased a shiny black five-speed Saab convertible. It was my "love at first sight" – a mental health escape, indeed. I drove whenever I could, the sun on my face and the wind in my hair, if only for a short while. This brought a sense of peace to my day. Rising early each morning, I intentionally walked five miles every day. I worked out, lifted weights, and did my best to eat a healthy diet. As a longtime cancer survivor, I knew taking care of myself was essential to my personal survival – especially under these stressful circumstances.

If I have learned anything from my journey, it is this: heartbreaking as it may seem, allowing a person their own struggle is always painful to witness, yet there is value in patience. Sometimes, struggles are exactly what we need in our lives. If we were to move through each day without obstacles, we would be crippled. We would not be as strong as we could have been. Give every opportunity a chance, leave no room for regrets, and don't forget the power of the struggle. This experience has been essential for my own recovery.

Remembering that addiction is a family disease and accepting that we are powerless over our addicted loved one is the first step. AND, while this is true, the substance user needs help and support. However, that is the job before them and their higher power, not ours.

I will not suffer in silence. Through education, I now understand that drug addiction is defined as a substance use disorder (SUD). I am working to manage my life in ways that bring personal change and a better way to live. For example, I have learned to develop personal boundaries and understand that detachment from my loved one(s) does by no means equal an absence of love.

With my "oxygen mask" in place, this means taking care of me. As my family's crises have passed from one to the next, I have developed tools and resilience as a result along this walk. And this is really how I am able to be here today to share my story with you.

Take pause for a moment. In recent weeks, you only have to step outside your front door, walk down your Main Street, listen to a radio or television station, or read a local newspaper to know that opiates, and deadly fentanyl too, have arrived in almost every town.

Perhaps you do not have an individual struggling with addiction in your family. You may not even be aware of addiction in a friend or acquaintance. This does not mean, however, that you are not affected by the outcomes of addiction. The path of destruction is plowing right through our own neighborhoods – yours and mine.

In 2016, I happened to watch a segment of CBS' *60 Minutes* with Scott Pelley reporting. During the hour-long show, Pelley interviewed Michael Botticelli, then-director of National Drug Control Policy.

"Addiction is a brain disease; this is not a moral failing. This is not about bad people who are choosing to continue to use drugs because they lack willpower. You know we don't expect people with cancer to stop having cancer," Botticelli said.

Pelley asked, "Aren't they doing it to themselves? Isn't a heroin addict making that choice?"

Botticelli replied, "Of course not. You know, the hallmark of addiction is that it changes your brain chemistry. It actually affects the part of your brain that's responsible for judgment."

Upon personal reflection, I admit that since that September day in 1998, my own deep anguish still surfaces from time to time. I have been unable to personally fulfill what I perceived as my role as a mother: the fixer, the one capable of stopping the personal siege of pain experienced by the people closest to me. Yet with the knowledge I have gained and with the help of God, who has been walking right alongside me, I am clearly able to live in recovery "one day at a time."

And although my partner Chris and I parted ways after a long go together, it goes without saying that I am forever grateful for her support and love, which continues even today for my grandchildren and me.

To paraphrase the poem "On Friendship" from our *NarAnon Blue Book* ...

The words you have heard here today are meant to offer hope, strength and encouragement. Please take what is worth keeping, and with a breath of kindness, blow the rest away.

~ *Chapter 4* ~

The Needle:
A Closer Look (1998-2002)

In my family's history, we had for many years enjoyed an annual excursion to Washington, D.C. with my mom and dad. I would travel from home, my sister Joan would come in from wherever she was living at the time, and we would spend three or four days together. Staying at the Hyatt near the Capitol was just wonderful family time. By then, my folks had retired to Arizona, then in later years to Albuquerque, New Mexico.

In September 1998, I invited Camille and Josh on this yearly trip. I was sure my daughter would be thrilled to have a short break from parenting. However, when they arrived at my front door to take the ride to the airport, I was shocked at what I saw. It wasn't my daughter standing there with the children, it was, my longtime childhood friend Rosemary (who, sadly, recently passed away, and whose son Michael, incidentally, first introduced Jamie to heroin). Josh appeared his usual self, but Camille was all made up and wearing big hoop earrings. I thought, *wow, this is really kind of odd*. At the time, the children were ages seven and nine, respectively.

For our Thursday departure, Chris was going to drive us to the airport, and we all got into the car. Once the kids were buckled in the back seat, they immediately started fighting, and I thought, *Mother of God, I have really put myself in a position here*. It was the worst ride of my life. They were immediately physically at each other, digging their fingernails into each other's arms and screaming hysterically. I couldn't believe it. I was looking at Chris and thinking, *Maybe you just want to turn this car around and go back home.* That was the second sign of trouble – the earrings, the makeup, and now this. Something was terribly wrong. Little did I know that these were the symptoms of a much larger picture yet to be revealed.

Trauma subsiding, we proceeded to our gate, boarding the plane and before we knew, we were greeting my parents at the Hyatt. Recalling our three days, we had a great, great time together. Just a word, with Mom in charge, it was her show; let's just say she never put up with goofy kid stuff. If you got "the look" or the raised eyebrow, that was your cue and you just knew that you had crossed the line.

With Dad part of our group, Joshua had a male family member with whom to bond. At the time of this particular trip, my son Greg was living in Virginia. He drove up for a day with his wife and their little boy, Andrew, who was about the same age as Josh. And, as I said earlier, despite the initial shock of departure, all in all, it was a wonderful experience.

Arriving back home, Jamie was supposed to meet up with us. Since I couldn't reach her, we decided to go to Pizza Hut and have something to eat. In the meantime, I continued to call. She finally responded, and when we finished our meal, we drove back to our home. She was inside – and I remember this so vividly, because in her life, it has always been all about her. She came out of the house in a rush, never saying hello to her children. Of course, they were very excited to see their mom, and probably really tired of being around me and their great-grandmother.

"You've got to listen to me!" she kept saying. "I'm in trouble. I'm really in trouble, and I need your help."

In Jamie's life, and I will go back to in utero, she has always been a mover. From the moment I started to feel her life inside of me, I felt constant motion. This was not anything anybody was concerned about at the time, but to go back and think about it, maybe there was something neurological going on – an imbalance or disturbance. She would constantly roll back and forth, back and forth. At birth, she was a big baby – eight and a half pounds.

I first became pregnant at eighteen, very shortly after Jerry and I married. Within weeks, I had a miscarriage. Six months later, I got pregnant again, and again...another miscarriage. I've often wondered if that wasn't the universe saying *maybe you need to just pay attention here, and not move forward with having children.* Yet, we persisted.

Gregory was born first, and then Jamie two years later. In her infancy, she refused to relax and sleep. She couldn't be comforted in any way, and it was very troubling to see that side of her, even when she was so young.

And so, when we returned from our trip, the drama, the agitated state, was really nothing new. During her childhood, my day could be destroyed while sitting at my desk at work just by getting a phone call from her. She would relay some kind of outrageous incident or story, and you know, I would be very codependent. The pattern with Jamie always has been very unsettling.

"Mom, I am a heroin addict," my daughter was saying to me now. "I have a bed, and I have treatment set up, but you need to take me there right now."

Wait? What? Jamie!

It was late. I had just come back from a long trip, and Chris needed to get up at four in the morning for work. We weren't expecting to have the children overnight, to say nothing of an extra day, but we stood to the challenge.

Jamie had indeed secured a bed at a hospital in a nearby town. I drove her there, but I don't recall the conversation. I think I was just kind of in a fog. What she was saying to me was that she had a detox facility lined up. I certainly didn't know what that meant – detox facility – yet. I would understand soon enough.

I knew I would have to get the kids ready the next day, then drive six miles to school in one direction, and another twelve miles in the opposite direction to work. The ensuing weeks became a logistical challenge as Chris and I tried to figure out how to make it all work. We became adept at spontaneity, believing this was only temporary. It took a little while to realize that this was something we would need to do over a period of time, while Jamie was where she needed to be to get better and come home.

Well, that didn't happen.

She ended up leaving her first rehab after 10 days, but not before I had the opportunity to attend a family session … Intro to Drug Addiction 101 – my first professional or academic exposure to the world of addiction. I don't remember any of the content, but I do remember being there, present and thinking, *What the Hell!*

I became immersed in caring for my grandchildren, and in what was happening at home with Chris holding the reins right along beside me. Jerry and I, long divorced, were once again thrown together, this time with a common purpose: to support one another. We didn't know what kind of a slippery slope we were on with Jamie, who by now was constantly calling and asking for money without any interest at all in what was going on with her children.

One day, while I was in conversation with the school principal, he said, "You know, these kids are no longer living in this school district, so, unfortunately, we're going to have to terminate their attendance here."

Okay.

Now I had to figure out how that was going to work, and

after numerous phone calls, questions with answers, I learned this first meant I needed to obtain legal guardianship for each of the children. With Jamie, we went to probate court to secure legal guardianship. I was also able to get permission from their dad, who lived in a neighboring state. Neither parent contested my request.

Learning the process was easy: apply for guardianship with our local probate court, obtain permission from both parents. Learning to live our new lives, on the other hand, would become the challenge of a lifetime.

In January 1999, with guardianship approved, Camille and Josh were once again enrolled in school within walking distance of home.

My focus remained on my ever-increasing responsibilities. For a time, we had little contact with Jamie. There were occasional phone calls: "I need money," that kind of thing.

Jerry and I gave in at first, and my daughter and her husband bought a car. Their life together was focused on using, so far as I knew; family was not part of her plan at that time.

As you will later read, there was a brief time when Jamie expressed interest in reclaiming her children – and she did. The results, however, were disastrous and short lived.

~ *Chapter 5* ~

Love is the Thread

What you are about to read are a series of actual letters, mostly between my ex-husband Jerry and me. The letters describe events and occurrences that took place in real time during the first four years of our daughter's known addiction to heroin. Selected from hundreds – yes, hundreds – of letters, I have attempted to choose those writings that most accurately reflect the painful and often unbelievable situations we faced as we did our best to ride out the storms, often hanging on with loose reins for dear life.

Don't try to add logic or make sense of these words, just read along as you have a front row seat, looking through our window into the world of full blown addiction – our family under the influence.

United in the face of unbelievable shock, worry and trauma – even an attempted reunion between Jamie and her children – Jerry and I created an unconditional support system for one another. We had no choice but to face this monumental challenge head on. In spite of the gravity of the challenges we were facing, we were there for one another…no matter what.

For the purposes of this book, the letters are presented not in traditional back-and-forth fashion, but as a narrative all their own, a jagged reflection of our disorientation and panic. Many of Jerry's responses to my letters came in the form of telephone calls, the content of which is now lost to time. Know that his support was strong, compassionate and unwavering. A few of my journal entries, along with letters to my daughter Jamie, my sister Joan, and Jerry's wife Judy are included here, as well. Like our own experience, their sequencing is uneven, imperfect, disjointed and fraught with tension.

Hope, ever so slight, always hope

Even though our hopes for Jamie's sobriety were nearly always dashed, once again we allowed ourselves emotion, excitement, giddy even, when we learned of her decision to return to her previous job – one where she had achieved great personal success. We were encouraged. Hope is always a wish.

November 1998

Hi Jerry,

Life just gets in the way when you're busy making other plans. Very hectic here, and difficult dealing with Jamie. She makes her financial demands very well known, to say the least. To bring you up to date, she called on Monday morning. Checks were bouncing for things like food, gas, and whatever else. She is no longer drinking or doing any drugs, to my knowledge, but she has the behavior of someone who does. Demanding, inconsistent, erratic, etc. She needs to be under clinical care, but I cannot make her do it.

I gave her money to cover her checks, but not before a very difficult conversation with her in person – in which she ripped me up and down for her awful childhood and how it felt to be her, wishing she had never been born, how you and I ruined her life, etc. I feel so disconnected from her as a person. She seems so unhappy and angry, and seems to feel that someone owes her something. I have made an attempt to talk with someone at a local mental health hospital. So far, we have missed each other, but I will keep trying.

She is not going back to her job as of yesterday. When she went to work on Monday morning, she was told she needed a medical release of which she was unaware. It was very upsetting to her and very disappointing, and certainly did not help our cause. She has decided to move with Matty to live with his mother, as long as they are both sober and clean. I have agreed to keep the kids through the school year.

The kids are missing their mother, especially Camille and on top of that, in tears one day recently, she told me the questions never stop from schoolmates who barrage her with questions like "why are you living with your grandmother, why don't you live in your own home with your mother?" And daily, out of frustration, she says, "my mother is dead."

So, you can see and understand why she has been quite a handful in the past few days, and yet, I am human, too, as I continue pulling out my hair over her. She is insolent, belligerent and uncooperative.

In part, I believe this stems from the visit they had over the weekend with Jamie. I don't know what she has told them, but somehow, indirectly, I think she has been undermining some of my efforts. She even asked Joshua for $20 so she could buy food. If that isn't just unbelievable, I don't know what is.

Josh starts therapy on Monday, and Camille the following Thursday. Camille is in need of help big time, and I know it won't correct her behavior overnight. I am so frustrated, tired and spent, but I don't know what else to do but keep going.

I got a call from Jamie yesterday, and she is very unhappy to be living with Matty – says he is very controlling and that she is going to leave. Of course, she wants to come and live with me, which I have nixed. I cannot do that. I'm hoping she will find someone that she can stay with. If she could understand that she needs to concentrate on herself, it would be the best thing for everyone.

Thanks again for your support. Give me a call, and we can talk some more.

Love, Annie

Hi Jerry,

Chris and I went to a friend's house for dinner and to celebrate her fiftieth birthday, getting home at about 9:55. The kids were actually in bed asleep, if you can imagine that. Jamie and Matty were here – she needed to talk to me. She said she had registered her car and that she needed me to put that amount into her account, plus car insurance of $230.

Jerry, do I understand from her that the money you have given me is only for her, as she says? I was under the impression that you were trying to help out with the kids, and that this money was not exclusively for her use. Please help me out here. I am putting the $711 that she paid for the registration into her account to cover the check. I did reiterate to her that we were not going to help her past this point, but she made some mention of the fact that she has been paying your car insurance for the past months, and feels she is due a reimbursement.

This is the latest pounding I am getting from her – that it is my fault she is where she is, because I wouldn't let her live with us after she came out of the hospital. If we continue to give her money, we are enabling her behavior, which helps her to stay addicted – not necessarily to drinking or drugging, but to the horrible behavior. She must know that we cannot cure her.

If there are any Al-Anon groups near where you live, Jerry, you might try one. It can be very helpful. Jamie will not be happy if we don't give her money, but it is the only way she is going to get better. When she can support herself and perhaps regain some dignity in her life, she will then – and only then – understand our decision. But you know what? I am not hopeful that she will make the right decision.

The latest word is that Camille and Josh must change schools because they no longer reside in their township. This will all happen after January 1. Believe it or not, neither of them is upset about it, and I guess I have only been worried because of yet another transition. So I will go with the flow, as they say, and think positively about this next step.

The holidays are rapidly approaching, and I've been able to do some shopping, though not on the same scale as in past years. My finances are very tight, not to mention the bills that I have as a result of Jamie's reckless behavior…a $175 telephone bill, for instance. She will pay this back to me, every penny, even if it is $10 a week. Anyway, so it goes.

I'm having a tough day today. I've been thinking about Jamie and how sad her situation is. I really feel that there is no way that she can have the children for a long time now, or ever. I have been having a meltdown of emotions that has me wanting my own life back. I just can't stop thinking about it over and over. Maybe it is the effects of hearing Matty say that her doctor had really bad news, knowing that she is really sick and incapable of taking care of herself or supporting herself, at least in the short term. I cannot imagine what it must feel like to be her. She has messed up royally, and now she knows it. I only wish she knew the ever-reaching tentacles of her actions. I appreciate your support, and know that you, too, are feeling much like I am at this point. Sad, but resigned, unfortunately.

Love, Annie

March 1999

Dear Joan,

As of Saturday, Jamie reclaimed her role as Camille and Joshua's mother, whether she was ready to do so or not. I felt as though I was coming unglued due to the stress, and needed to act quickly. The frenzy that follows Jamie is very hard to avoid.

When she is near, my telephone is ringing off the hook: new AA and NA friends, and, as you know, Jamie cannot function without a telephone. Matty calling, Mike calling…you get the idea. Anyway, I had a meltdown of sorts, and felt that my sanity was at risk. I needed to reclaim my life immediately.

Chris and I had just returned from a wonderful vacation in Key West, during which time Jamie and Jerry had stayed at my place with the kids. When we came back, Jerry left immediately and Jamie was more or less around, in and out but basically staying with a friend. I began to feel it was really her responsibility at that point, and that I was not going to be put in a position of just being a full-time babysitter. The more time she spent at our house, the less control I had of my own space, and the kids really wanted to be with Jamie.

Since then, I have had a sense of free moments to breathe. It does seem as though it has been a long, long time in coming. I went to a meditation retreat last Sunday, and had a hard time sitting still for lengths of time, although the peace and solitude of it was very refreshing.

The past several weeks have found me experiencing many different emotions over the children going back. Sadness and loss, and then happiness and relief. I'm in a place that is hard to explain.

It feels good not to be on the run to school and appointments, preparing the same meals: cheeseburgers, pizza, or pork chops for a fussy crowd. But in all fairness, I do miss them. I am taking full advantage of having my own time, even just staying home on the weekends, but I also feel as though I have somewhat abandoned them, too.

Jamie has been staying at a motel, which is owned by Rosemary and somewhat frequented by Mike. I have not talked with her very often since that Saturday. I'm afraid of what will happen. On the one hand, I don't really want to know. On the other, I have tried to meet with her, but so far, we have not connected.

Matty was sentenced to prison for two years for his part in an incident in January. As far as I know, Jamie is still working on getting a divorce from him so she can marry Mike, maybe. Who knows? It is a sad state of affairs.

Love, Annie

Hi Jerry,

For a time, I really did not have much communication with Jamie. She was very vague at times, then accusatory and paranoid. My suspicion was that she was using again.

The school principal and I have had a series of conversations over the past several months, and there seems to be a very big problem with the children getting to school on time, if it all. Out of 17 days, they were late 16. This is not setting a very good example for them, and it is seriously concerning the school. Since I have legal guardianship, I'm still in the loop, and ultimately responsible. My main focus is the kids and what is best for them. At times, it appears that Mike is the responsible one in picking them up from school, because Jamie just "forgets" to do it.

Yesterday, since I was unable to raise Jamie, I decided to drive to Mike's home to see what was up. I pulled in, and her car was not there. I knocked on the slider, as I could see the TV was on, and then saw her on the couch. I knocked again, and she said, "Come in." The door was locked, which I tried in order to let her know. She finally opened the door and let me in. Long story short, she has been using again since January 20, the day after your mom died. The good news is that we had a very constructive adult conversation in which I laid out the facts: if she didn't get her act together, I was certain she would be in jeopardy of losing her children or her life. She heard every word I said, and when she started to get argumentative, I told her I would not be part of an argument. I told her that I was there as her friend, not her mother. Let me tell you, that really helped me get through the conversation, especially because I feared the worst upon arriving at the house – that I would, in reality, find her dead.

She called me at around 8:45 p.m. last night, and said that she had thought about our conversation and realized what she needed to do. She asked me to take the kids, which I agreed to do if she was able to find a program to get into. We talked for about 45 minutes. She was feeding the kids their supper and talking to me at the same time. We said goodbye after I suggested that she find a program that would take Medicaid.

Jamie called me at 6:15 this morning to say that she had found a place mid-state that would take her with a referral. She was going to try to get a referral through a local recovery agency, but apparently decided to try the hospital first. She called from the emergency room of our local hospital, saying that she had gone there in hopes of getting a physician to refer her, which she was able to do. Chris and I went to the ER to stay with her until she had been taken care of, then came back and talked.

She was high again, having used earlier in the morning. She admitted to shooting up at 6 a.m. She was feeling no pain, and was willing to go through the pain that will come in the next several days as she goes through withdrawal again.

After she took a shower, we did her errands, had some lunch, and came back here. I needed to pick up Josh and Camille from school, and Jamie needed to go to Mike's to pack her things. Chris and I were going to take her to her next detox bed, but Mike decided that he wanted to take her, so she went along with him. They should be there by now.

Jamie said goodbye to Camille this morning, but waited to say anything to Josh until his school day was over, which was a good thing. He seemed okay with it. At this point, everyone is covered for the day. I have told Jamie that this is the last time I will be able to help her, and that she needs to complete this program – and if she doesn't, she pretty much knows what the results will be.

After her detox, which was nine days last time, she can receive calls between 3:30 and 10 p.m. I will let you know what the patients' number is as soon as I can. I'll be around tonight and throughout the weekend. I remain optimistic, and I know Jamie will be trying.

Love, Annie

May 1999

Hi Jerry,

Rosemary has the children, taking them yesterday afternoon for an overnight and bringing them back tonight. She has been available this time, which has been helpful. When she came by yesterday, we had a chance to talk while the kids had their lunch. The news is not good, unfortunately.

Mike and Jamie came back into town on Thursday. Jamie has dyed her hair black. Mike's is orange and yellow. Apparently, they had clean time away, but once they got back into town, they went out drinking, and according to Rosemary, Jamie found her way back to some drug activity. I said, "Well, at least I know now what I have to do." Sad though it is, I know that I will not be able to count on her, and will now count her out of the plan. By the way, she has not called here to say that she is back.

So for now, that is where I am – just moving forward instead of sitting on my hands waiting for a miracle. I hope that you can somehow detach yourself from what our daughter has done to herself and her family. She really isn't the same person, though I guess we know that she has been troubled for some time. This has really put her over the edge, however. Last night I prayed that the misery that she was suffering here on Earth could somehow be alleviated by an extraterrestrial force. I continue to hope that will happen, because this hell she is living is one that is incomprehensible to most. With a success rate of 4 in 100, the odds do not look good, considering her desire to drug herself.

Love, Annie

Hi Jerry,

It's Sunday morning, Camille's birthday.

Jamie got very drunk on Thursday night, waking up at Mike's, not knowing where she was. Apparently, according to them both, she blacked out. He took her to the emergency room at the hospital when he couldn't get her to wake up. I found all of this out on Friday morning, having made arrangements previously to take the day off and also to have her pick up the kids at school. They were looking forward to that. Well, you can imagine, with all of that information, I was beginning to suspect that she might not make it to school at all.

Earlier in the day, Jamie had promised she would be there, but she was so totally off the wall when I spoke with her. She and Mike were also going to go to a local breeder to buy a Jack Russell puppy for Camille's birthday gift, and then to pick the kids up at school. Well, 3 o'clock came, and no Jamie. Chris picked up the kids and brought them back home. Around 4:00, Mike and Jamie showed up with their mountain bikes in tow. Apparently, they had gone to pick up the puppy, but it was already sold. Jamie had called the school to say that "the kids' grandmother" was going to pick them up that day…I wonder who that was, since I had already told her I would be on my way to the airport to pick up my dad. In the end, the kids went with her for the weekend late Friday afternoon, and I have not talked with her since early Friday morning.

In any case, Camille now has the Jack Russell puppy, which she named Lucky. Lucky stays at Mike's during the school week. Another one of Jamie's tricks, trying to convince me to take the dog so that Camille will not be sad to leave her dog until her next visit. Of course, Camille was elated, but the lengths to which Jamie had to go to get it were unbelievable. She doesn't have any money, so I don't know how she paid for it.

Did I tell you about the meeting I had with Rosemary, Mike, and Jamie on May 12? I called a meeting to discuss summer plans, since Jamie and Mike are very adamant about having the kids live with them from that point on. I arrived at the restaurant where we were meeting to find Jamie already there, with a drink in hand. Overall, it was very productive, despite the fact that Mike was late by about one and a half hours, feigning that he didn't realize the important nature of the meeting. My objective, of course, was to try to get them to understand the seriousness of their behavior and how it is affecting all of us. Since Mike wasn't there initially, I talked with Jamie to try to instill the importance of setting some goals – even simple ones. Finally, she decided that the most important goal would be to avoid getting high, with which I certainly agreed. She also said she needed to go to her noon meetings daily and make a commitment to herself to do that.

Mike and Rosemary finally showed up. Rosemary had been there, but went to retrieve Mike when he called to say he needed a ride. I basically said that they were in deep jeopardy of losing the children permanently, and that Jamie could very easily have lost her parental rights by now, had I not been in the picture. It seemed to make some impact on all of them, but Mike will never fully understand this or his negative influence on our family.

During the meeting, I discussed a local residential treatment program again with Jamie. She at least listened this time, but she is definitely against going into this. She is, unfortunately, addicted to Mike, and until she really hits bottom, nothing is going to change, I'm afraid.

We concluded the meeting agreeing to meet again in three weeks (that will be this week.) Now, let me tell you what Jamie has done in response to the goals she set up. I believe she is straight and has not been getting high, but her behavior resembles that of someone who has been using and drinking. Up and down, and of course, the night after our meeting, she went out, got drunk, and passed out. She was found on the floor at her house in a puddle of urine. Lovely thought, isn't it?

My job situation is tenuous, at best. I met with the new president, whose office is in Connecticut. They are offering a severance package of one week's pay for each year I worked. I could take the summer off, rest my head, and try to figure out what I will do next.

Love, Annie

September/October 1999

Hi Jerry,

For once, I believe I have some encouraging news regarding Jamie. Short version: through the efforts of the school and Joshua's 504 Plan eligibility, her family will qualify for a great deal of assistance through state and federal funding. Whatever counseling services they need can be provided, and, most importantly, support for Jamie when she gets "stressed" will also be there for her. She will be given the number for a hotline if things get to be too much for her, and she needs to be in touch with someone who can give her some advice and resolve. There are one-on-one aides to assist with both Camille and Josh. Finally, this gets me out of the unpleasantness of constantly pushing her to make decisions, and, as she says, being hard on her. I can be a grandmother once again. No more blaming Mom.

Then I saw Jamie on Monday afternoon at the grocery store. I thought she looked as if she were using again – pale, sunken eyes, scabs around her mouth. Prior to my seeing her, I received a telephone call from Rosemary. She was concerned about the kids in terms of their welfare, and the activities in which she suspected Jamie was involved again. She said that Jamie had scored more heroin, and had wanted to share it with Mike's brother. Of course, I was upset to hear this news, not only because of its effect on the children, of course, but also because I was dealing with my last day on the job on Thursday, and still thinking a great deal about a situation with my parents. I listened to her unsurprised, and decided to take a wait-and-see approach. As you can imagine, when I saw Jamie on Monday, her appearance confirmed what Rosemary had told me.

This morning, at 8 o'clock, I got a message from one of Jamie's friends saying to call her, that it was an emergency. Apparently, she had convinced Jamie to go into rehab again, so on Monday afternoon she took her quite willingly to a place this time out of state to begin treatment. Unfortunately, Jamie left there last night, signing herself out at around 8:30. She had no money, no car, no checks, credit cards, or clothes – only what she was wearing, which I understood to be pajamas.

She ended up in a town south of us and managed to score drugs and alcohol, which, according to her friend, she proceeded to use all night long. As I have tried to explain to you in past weeks, this is about her mental illness, and, in my opinion, the drug and alcohol addiction is secondary to that. She needs to get help for the illness, and all of the AA meetings and rehabilitation centers are not going to do her any good until the mental illness is identified diagnosed and prescribed with medication.

Jamie's friend convinced her to go back into rehab: another place close to where she had been admitted earlier in the week. She is there, or at least we think she is there, as of this afternoon at 1:00. What's different about this place is that it is a locked facility at least for 72 hours after admittance. The patient must readily admit herself with the understanding that she cannot leave for at least that long. We will be faced with convincing her that she must do this for herself and for her family.

Let's talk about this after you get a chance to digest it all. For now, that's about it. I'll keep you informed from this end.

Love, Annie

November 1999

Dear Annie,

I received your letter, and I do agree with you: Jamie has to let the past go, and focus on today's elements. Easy to say, but alas...hard to do.

I know Jamie does a number on you, and I've told her many times she's wrong. What she is doing right now is much worse than any supposed happenings before, and with much more tragic results.

It's hard to treat Jamie the same as before. We can try, and I have stressed to her that we love her and are just trying to help her. I tried to convey that she needs to help, which I know she knows, deep down. Sad to say, Jamie's life has affected us both greatly in the past year, and of course, we have both told truths which she ignored, but which proved to be accurate forecasts.

One more thing, Annie – be assured that I am not going against any advice you give Jamie, or disagreeing with you at all. No way is she going to say that we have different ideas. I do think that if she can work, she should try – after getting treated for the bipolar, her using, and getting well under the advice of a doctor or counselor.

I wish the year 2000 to be better for us all – Jamie first, of course. As she goes, we can go too, I think. Thanks for all you're doing. Annie, please don't feel like shit. We all do things, and no one is perfect. You're a good person, and I know you know it, but I'll say it to you, and I mean it.

I guess that's all for now. Please advise me about the plans. I feel like no more financial help until Jamie goes to the psychiatrist and gets proper help.

Love, Jerry

Hi Jerry,

Don't know if you heard, but Jamie's car was repossessed yesterday. I got a message from her this morning with this latest news. When I stopped at her house last Saturday with groceries to fill her cupboards, someone from the bank called, so obviously, it was only a matter of time.

I believe she sees that everything is falling apart, and if it were not for her family, and, God forbid, Mike, helping out, I don't know where she and the kids would be. We still need to talk with her about money management ASAP, and let her know ahead of time when we will sit down and talk with her. So, when you figure out a date in December when you will be coming here, please let me know.

Nothing can really be resolved at this moment, I know, but it is so damn frustrating. That is the hardest part in all of this… waiting for her to really fall flat.

I'll talk with you soon.

Love, Annie

Hi Annie,

I told Jamie that we love her and are trying to do our best for her. She said she knows you and I are there for her, and she appreciated that. She loves us, she said, so that's good…and yes, God forbid, Mike is helping. With the car gone, reality might set in somewhat, if that's not too depressing for her. But I think with the first of the month coming and welfare kicking in, hopefully...

Love, Jerry

December 1999

Hi Jerry,

Glad you connected with Jamie. I don't know much about methadone per se, other than it is a form of treatment for heroin addicts. It would appear that some of its effects mirror the real thing: tiredness, etc. I only know that I'm glad she is making an attempt at something positive. The program she's considering is expensive, and not covered under Medicaid. Our state has some legislation about allowing methadone clinics in the state, but so far, it has been shot down.

I agonize over what is best. Should I leave her alone and let her run her life the way it plays out, or do I somehow figure out a way for intervention? Then, who would be the person or persons to coordinate this effort, and what would the success rate be? It kills me that she continues to stay at Mike's primarily, because the atmosphere surrounding her is not a safe environment. I remain in the grips of not knowing what to do, for the most part, and try to take care of myself as the first priority.

The children seem to be riding it out again. Both of them are doing well, and to Jamie's credit, they are getting to school and are being picked up on time. I believe she does need to get Josh in to see his pediatrician.

I'm afraid my day was not as productive as I would have liked it to have been. I spoke with Jamie last night and told her that I would drop by sometime today – which, at the time, was okay by her, as long as it was after Mike had left for work. So I fashioned my day around that. She had apparently had a rough day with Mike, who was driving fast to the clinic and telling her to jump out of the car, end her life, that sort of thing. This stuff is craziness, and yet she's stuck. She won't move. All she wants to do is sleep and escape it.

Enter the psychiatrist. Unfortunately, Jamie has only seen her once, and has not made an appointment with a local therapist, as recommended by the psychiatrist. I really need your help to try to convince her of what is best for her and the children. I know she cares about her animals, but dogs and cats cannot come first. Anyway, I told her that I had gotten some legal advice about her bankruptcy, and asked her to put together a list of all her bills. She said she would. I also asked her to promise that she would call that local women-only residential program, which she said she would do, too.

The good news is that the clinic has begun to reduce her dosage, so she is not sleeping as much, but as she says it's just money in the government's pocket, this legal methadone thing. I believe it, too. I don't even know if they have an apartment available right now, but I pray that they might.

Love, Annie

January 2000

Hi Jerry,

I had asked Jamie several times to stop over to take a look at these legal forms for the meeting with the attorney today. She never bothered to do that. When I called her at 11:30 today, she had forgotten all about it. I was angry to hear that. I tried to be civil, and told her that when she decided she wanted to do something about it, she could get back to me. She told me she was "sick," so I called the attorney's office and canceled. Now, just a few minutes ago, I got a call from Jamie saying that her tire was flat, and could I pick up the kids and also buy her a package of cigarettes. She also said, "You don't have to come in when you drop the kids, if you don't want to."

I cannot win with her. She put me in a very awkward position. She wants everything, but she doesn't want to do anything we want her to do. So yes, I am picking up the kids, and I'm going to give her the following letter.

Dear Jamie,

Your father and I are doing our part in trying to help you and your current situation. By this, I mean that when we say we will do something, we come through — for example, putting money into your checking account when asked to. Again, we are willing to do whatever we can; however, in fairness, we are not inclined to offer our help when you do not do as you say you will. It is disheartening when you don't follow through on promises. We must insist on equality, which means we will meet you halfway. This is a ground rule we must follow. I want you to give this serious consideration.

With love, Mom

I'll talk with you soon.

Love, Annie

Hi Annie,

What I'm thinking is to have another talk with someone at the local residential program to see if it's possible to meet with her. You and I can get all the details, maybe meet with this other psychiatrist and get an idea from them about how strongly we can present this.

I think Jamie needs to be told that this is the time to act. I think the thing to do is try to meet with Jamie and really assess her motivation at this point, or try to motivate her. My feeling is, it's got to be soon. If not, we've lost.

Maybe I can come up and talk with you, Annie, and try to get Jamie to meet with us. We'll map a plan and try to implement it with her. One question comes to mind.

Where are the kids when Jamie goes to this detox for 7 to 10 days? What are your thoughts?

Take care,

Love, Jerry

February 2000

Hi Jerry,

I finally connected with Jamie today, and I know she is not feeling well, undoubtedly coming off the methadone. My conversation with her today was somewhat productive; however, she has to be the one to make the choice about going into detox, and there isn't anything anyone can say to her (or do for her) until she makes that choice.

She mentioned the other day that I could have her arrested. Well, okay, let's say I do that. She gets locked up for 30 days, comes out not yet ready to face the world clean and sober – then what? Suppose she goes out for more drugs? Now she has a record, and she is still using drugs, so the way I see it is to reinforce positive steps. She is staying clean for the moment, but is obviously agitated. I have encouraged her to go into detox. She has to do it. As I said in our meeting last week, there is no more discussion right now about the FIR program or forcing her to do what she does not want to do. She has to be ready, and this is what I believe. So, as they say, "let go and let God." I will be there for her, and will do whatever I can when she is ready – and only then, as I know you will. Trying to cajole her into detox will not work, so I hope we can all remember that, and for now, keep it as a priority if the time seems right and intervention can be put into place.

I'm incredibly sad about our family situation. I had Camille for a visit yesterday – picked her up at 10:30 and took her for breakfast. We did errands and a little shopping and had some fun, but it takes everything I have to not break down when I'm with her. She looks so sad, and tries to put up a good front.

She asked if she could spend the night, which she did. She called Jamie to ask if she could, but before she even asked, Jamie asked her to ask me if she could spend the night anyway. She went right to sleep, and slept nearly twelve hours. She got up around 9:30, had some breakfast, and then we went to church. She seemed to like being there…I know I did.

I took her home, and when I got there, Mike was just leaving and came back to give Jamie a hug. I don't know if that was for my benefit. Jamie wasn't making good eye contact with me, but I didn't know if that meant anything or not. I asked her if she was taking the medication, and she said she was. I didn't stay long, as she wasn't entirely communicative.

The biggest thing is that she is about to lose her driver's license. Too many points. Mike has already lost his. I'm really beside myself over this, as she says she will just drive illegally. This is just not responsible thinking, and I really don't know what to do with this information.

I have a splitting headache tonight, and feel like my heart is about to drop out of my body. She just doesn't see her behavior as anything other than what it is. And what about the long-term effects of her behavior on these kids? They deserve much more than this, and they need to get to school legally.

Love, Annie

Hi Joan,

Just by chance, Jamie called me yesterday afternoon and said that she was ready to go into a local detox program. The admissions director called the women's residential program and said they could interview her there, for the sake of convenience. She told him she was ready, and he agreed to make the necessary arrangements.

Today, she called me with discouraging news. Apparently, because of her failed attempts at detox and recovery, her reputation is following her, and because of this, they do not feel she is a good candidate with prospects for success. As I said to Jerry earlier today, you finally get the horse to the stream, but give it a straw with holes to drink from. She was offered another center north of us. Jamie now has that information, and with God's help, she will take the initiative to get there.

I won't know any more until tomorrow, so, my dear sis, you can see why I was lucky enough to lose my job, because this has been full-time employment right in my own house. You can probably tell it is more than discouraging, and as I'm sure you know, we cannot want her recovery more than she does. Unfortunately, she has done some irreparable damage to the children, and it breaks my heart to think about it.

Love, Annie

Hi Jerry,

I got a call from Jamie around noon time today. She was calling to say she didn't have any money. I told her that we had offered suggestions as to how she could be helping herself. She said she didn't call for a lecture, and wanted to know where you were: "Well, Dad can take trips and you can go to Florida, but you can't help me?" I said that we had offered her alternatives in the context of which we would help her. At that point, she hung up on me.

Please let me know what you think.

Love, Annie

Hi Annie,

I don't know what to say. If she would call me, I'd like to talk to her – when I call, I get Mike. He says she's sleeping. If she comes on, she never wants to talk much. I know she's hurting, but still, if she would be considerate and not demanding, it would be a much better tactic. I will try to call her today.

Is Mike, in fact, working? I have no interest in helping him. I am lost as to what to do. Are we not supposed to have some life? Also, if Jamie would follow through on some things, it would be easier. I know you agree. Tough love, I guess. It's no good to keep giving her money when we don't know where it's going. What do the "professionals" say is the best thing for us to do? What's their experience in how to go about these things?

Take care.

Love, Jerry

Annie's Journal

February 17, 2000

Mike spoke of Jamie using, and not being able to get up in the morning to attend to the kids – sometimes not even taking them to school at all.

He is now no longer working, and is staying home to make sure the kids get to school and are picked up on time. He is making two meals a day at home. He admitted to his own drug use, and to getting Jamie involved, as well. He wants to make a commitment to help the kids, but also needs to get a job.

He said he wanted to help Jamie because he felt guilty about what he had gotten her involved in, and felt compelled to do the right thing and try to get her into treatment.

Jerry wants to pursue psychiatric evaluation and committal. Can we do this? We believe she may harm herself. One of the children told me Jamie had tried to slit her wrists.

February 18, 2000

Jamie is threatening suicide. I called our women's crisis center, and they suggested calling the crisis team. I spoke with an advocate on the crisis line, explained my concerns, and was told to call the police.

Today, Jamie said, "I attempted suicide three times this week. There is no sense in living if I cannot have my children." At 12:45, I placed a call to the police to report my concerns and request a safety check at Jamie's house. They were supposed to call me back, but never did.

Dear Judy,

Things are not going exactly as planned, unfortunately. Jamie went to the hospital to have her blood drawn for her impending detox admission. While she was there, Mike arrived. The plan was that he would then go home and wait for a call to come pick Jamie up. However, they went first to meet with Rosemary to have lunch. By the time they got there, according to Rosemary, Jamie was drinking, saying that she would go to Burke Place, but she wouldn't stay. Begging her for money to buy drugs and begging Mike to take her south of the border for the same. He said no, he wouldn't do that.

I guess they got into a heated argument. She left me a message saying only that Mike was taking her to the program, and to tell the children that she loved them, saying "I hate you and Chris" before hanging up.

I told Jerry, and he is pretty discouraged. He left here to go to Mike's to see if they were there. Meanwhile, Rosemary called me back to say that after she paged Jamie, Mike did call her to say that they were on their way to detox, but that Jamie had tried to jump out of the car. He is going to call Rosemary when they arrive, and if she is willing to stay, which I doubt.

Annie

Hi Jerry,

Here is the latest synopsis of a conversation that I had last night with Jamie. She called around 6:30 while I was making dinner, and I asked her to call back at 9:30. From the onset of the conversation, she seemed coherent and rational, speaking in a normal tone without anger or threat. As the story goes, she stayed at detox for three days, and was then picked up by a friend, going to her house to stay. She called Mike, who said he was not going to talk to her until she got better. She then went out of state to another facility for two days because her blood pressure was too low, which runs on my side, as well. They would not give her medication. There was no TV, it was too hot...she left hitchhiking, I guess back to using eight to ten bags a day, now down to two to five.

She is using Valium (obtained from Rosemary) to help her come down. She predicts that with the help of the Valium, she will be clean by March 7. Mike is also getting clean, and will soon be done with methadone. They're looking into a local out-patient rehab program.

The whole time she was talking, I didn't interrupt her – only acknowledged what she was saying without prejudice. She said that she wants to see the children, and wants all of them to go back to therapy with Mike. She plans to move out of the house using her tax money, and is still thinking about the women's residential treatment program. Apparently, they have found someone to rent the house. She didn't know that the program wouldn't allow Mike to live with her! I didn't respond to that, but I did tell her that she could live there alone in anticipation of the kids joining her when she was clean.

I asked her how she was getting money for the heroin. She said she was hocking stuff: TV, VCR, Joshua's boom box. She wanted to know why I was asking that, thinking perhaps that I thought she was "hooking." I said I was only asking a question about obtaining money – no implied thoughts. She said that she had a dream night before last in which she, Josh, Mike, and myself were in some water trying to grab at life rafts. In it, she had Josh by the arm and grabbed at a raft, but it disappeared into thin air. She dropped down and died, and then saw her body, feeling no more pain.

I talked with her about the children's missed and tardy days at school. She said there were a couple of days when she had kept them home and shouldn't have. Last month was really bad for her, and she wanted to ask me to take the kids, but was afraid I wouldn't do it – afraid of rejection. She knows she doesn't have any chances left to get her act together.

She again reiterated her desire to get clean. Many issues to resolve from 20 years ago, but that needs to be put aside until she gets better. She said she can go for 36 hours without heroin, and then the desire becomes too great. She said she wished she had stayed at her last detox. At that point, I suggested that she call the local mental health hospital about helping her to go back and try again, and said that they would support her effort to do the right thing. She said she would think about it.

She knows things got really bad, and she needs a safe environment in which to live. She knows that she was hurting the children, and she has to live with that every day. I said her main concern was to get clean alone – that Mike should not be a part of her plan. We discussed her addiction to Mike, which she acknowledged. I promised that the children would be with me, and that I would keep them so they could all move into a larger place when she is clean, sober, and well. Then we would look at the next step.

Love, Annie

March 2000

Hi Joan,

Last week, during school vacation, I decided to drive to Virginia with the children for a visit with Greg and his family. Everyone had a very nice time, and it was wonderful to get a breather from the unpredictability of our lives. The kids enjoyed each other's company.

In my last email, I told you that the kids were going to live with their father. Well, that has now changed, and Chris and I have decided to take on the task of keeping them with us. I know it is a huge undertaking, but someone has to do it. They have been through so many emotional ups and downs in the past few years, and we think it best that they stay with us so there can be consistency, and so they can be with family, not in foster care. One of the other reasons they're not going to their father's house is that he lives in another state. There is no reciprocity between states for the services we have worked so hard to enlist: school counselors, special ed programs, that kind of thing. He was disappointed with our decision, but in the long run, I'm hoping this will be a win-win for everyone. He will participate as much as he can, taking them on the weekends and probably sometime in the summer.

I think they're making a good adjustment, but that is not to say that they do not miss Jamie. She has become entirely incapable of taking care of them, and they have seen the worst of it all – the details of which you can probably imagine. At different times, they have emotional outbursts about wanting their mother. We all want her back, but only as she was a long time ago. I think they have good memories of her, and try to hold onto those, and that is what they miss. We are going to return to family therapy. Both Camille and Joshua have counselors through their school, and both of them benefit from it. They really need to express their thoughts on their loss and anger, almost as if Jamie is really gone for good.

Jerry is bent on getting Jamie committed into rehab of some kind, but we know that this is something that is always voluntary, and the patient can leave at any time. She has been in eight different situations, walking every time. I say she is not ready. Jerry is concerned that if she continues, she will be dead before she can get well. She has tried suicide, cutting her wrists on more than one occasion. Her therapist has diagnosed her with borderline personality disorder based upon his visits with her and her actions in the past several months. It is so frustrating and heartbreaking to feel so helpless.

Jamie and Mike went to South Carolina again to try and dry out. I don't know if that was successful. I hear they're back. She has sold most of her tangible goods. In my last conversation with her, she said she was waiting for her IRS refund so they could move back to South Carolina. There was some talk about a bad drug deal, and that people were unhappy with Mike… people with guns who mean business.

Jamie was recently arrested driving on the interstate. The police found heroin, paraphernalia, etc., and she has to go to court tomorrow. Jamie said she was cooperative upon arrest, and is hoping for leniency. I am hoping that as part of her sentencing, they will mandate rehab, but I don't know what happens in that state for first offenders. If you can offer any info, I would appreciate it.

Love, Annie

April 2000

Hi Annie,

First, I need to say – and of course, you expect me to – accusations aside – I never abused Jamie. I am sure we had some words. As you know, she was always independent. That's why she came to live with me in the first place so many years ago, she was 12 at the time… always her style being independent. But honestly, I spent more time coming home from work trying to keep her happy – you remember the horse thing and taking her to lessons. But it's in the past now, and I can assure you that nothing physical happened at all.

I'll have to sleep on this some. I am distressed to have that said. It seems so hard to believe that Jamie thinks no one is ever there for her. I know you were always there. I guess we can't dwell on these things.

For now, I think any power other than us might help make Jamie more aware of her situation. I was really hoping that wanting her kids back would provide her with enough motivation, but alas, I don't think so. I think having the kids so young put a lot of pressure on her. Some feel they are robbed of their young lives, but it comes back to the fact that it was their choice.

If I can, and Jamie wants me to, I'd be glad to come and go to court with her. I do think we have been allowing Jamie some choice, but we need to try to have it be her choice, too. If she wants to go into a program, I'd be willing to try to help that way.

I think you're doing great, and that everything you are doing will help the kids a lot in the long run.

Love, Jerry

"We seem to be powerless to do anything at all." – Jerry

Hi Jerry,

Just thought I would let you know that I got a call early yesterday from Jamie, but didn't talk to her until last night. I will give you the short version. Several days ago, she left Mike's and went to south to her new friends. As of last night, she was five days clean with the help of her new "friends," a family she has met recently. She called me because she wanted me to call her therapist to ask if he would still see her, and maybe give her the antipsychotic drug he prescribed for her back in December.

Of course you know that this puts me in an awkward position, but I agreed that I would try to reach him for her. I talked with him first thing this morning, and he is willing to work with her, but don't get your hopes up for him to see her again. She has to make contact with one of the local programs, at which point he said that he would be glad to see her right away. He also told me that she could call and get on the waiting list for an appointment.

When I passed this information along to her today, she was understanding of why he couldn't just drop everything to see her. I explained that she had very poor credibility with him, and that she needed to basically start over in the present and forget about the past. She said she would call him, but then in the next breath, she said she is no longer living locally, so maybe she would get a new doctor altogether. You can kind of see where I'm going with this. I believe she's clean, but she is also exhibiting hypomania, and in my experience with her, she jumps from one subject to the next without listening to anything that is being said.

Jamie asked me to come and pick her up and take her to Mike's to get some clothes, and last night, she asked me to go and check on her dog. She now has another puppy – a total of three dogs. I told her I just couldn't do that. She asked me to call Rosemary, and again, I told her that I just couldn't do that, either. She told me that she had called the police to escort her to the house so she could get some clothes. I told her that I would help her, but I'm a little concerned about going to his house and getting even more involved … far more than I ever intended to be.

That is where it stands from here. Give me your thoughts. I would welcome them. The kids are fine. Camille is canoeing today with her outdoor group, and Joshua has been inside working on his scrapbook of our New Mexico trip. I am holding up, but this Jamie thing is absolutely unbelievable. She's really out there, and while I want to believe her, I believe she thinks that what she says is the way it is. We have all been there before with her. I hope she continues to maintain her ability to stay clean. That would be a step in the right direction.

Love, Annie

"I don't think she can just walk away or use these people like she has used others in the past without severe consequences. In fact, I am now more than concerned about my own safety." – Annie

"Make sure your doors are locked." – Jerry

May 2000

Hi Jerry,

In talking with Jamie today, I could hear that she is really trying to do the right thing and wants our approval. She said she would submit to testing to prove that she was clean. She also said that the people she is staying with are very nice, clean, and living in a good place – and that I shouldn't worry about her.

She is spending time with Luis: thirty years old, works out. I don't know if he works at a job, however. She says he has been very helpful in getting her clean. I told her that I applaud her efforts, and realize how hard it must be for her. I also said I needed to see more, now that she was making the right choice, and that she needed to see a doctor, get to some meetings, and get into therapy immediately. It is her choice, at this point.

I heard her say that she's going to stay there and try to get established, maybe with this person she's talking about. Of course, this reminds me a little of the time she got involved with Matty, and you know what happened there.

So, this morning has been really tough on me, especially when I told her that I would not drive to see her and that we all have to make our choices. I thought I was being supportive by taking care of the children, but she is still offended when I say this to her.

I just wish this would not continue – swirling around in a sea of emotion. You know what? I hung up on her. I know she was upset. I was crying and trying to maintain my composure, but you just can't imagine what this does to me. When I called her back, she did give me the number of where she is staying. Her pager has been disconnected. I was still crying. I think she understood my conflict about not wanting to see where she is. She tried to assure me that it was a nice place, not full of cockroaches, etc. She said she realized that it was hard for me. I told her that I would either send her things on the bus or meet her somewhere in between. She's going to call me back and let me know how we can make this happen.

Love, Annie

Hi Jerry,

Jamie is back in town with Luis, staying with a friend last night. She called yesterday to say they are looking for a car, as Luis managed to get some cash – $1,100 from someplace. She said she wouldn't bother me – wouldn't ask for money or to see the kids, just wanted to let me know that she was okay, which is okay with me. However, I need these conversations to be short, with no recriminations toward others – you, for example.

She called again and left a message last night:

"Just to let you know, we bought a car, 1986 Honda Prelude

from the Chrysler garage here in town, $900 includes insurance, registration, etc."

They had $200 left over. Don't know where the cash came from – she didn't say. Then she said they were on their way home. Don't know where that is today. I'm continuing to move forward with the NarAnon chapter, which will meet Tuesday, June 6, in a meeting room at a local bank. I am making a lot of contacts, and feel this will be a good thing for the community, not to mention myself.

Just a note on methadone treatment ... our state has passed a bill to provide methadone in a hospital setting now. This is good news, but it won't take effect until the guidelines are in place, which is supposed to be by December 31, 2000. At least it is a start in the right direction.

Love, Annie

Hi Annie,

A little news. As you know, Jamie has been calling, asking for assistance in renting an apartment ($500 with a $500 deposit), but as I told you, I don't have it, and you don't agree with doing that anyway. So, more ensuing phone calls. I suggested, "Why not look at something smaller and cheaper until you can get a paycheck? I know they have weekly rates at motels."

In fact, she did that, and called me. So, probably to your dismay, I agreed to pay for one week at $195. I talked to the owner, and told him I wouldn't use the credit card; I'd send a check. He said okay. I called the police to check on the address, and they confirmed it was a motel. I also called directory assistance and got the same data Jamie had given me, but in the same breath, she told me there was a $50 deposit, which was news to me. I told Luis I wasn't paying any deposit. He said there was no deposit, that Jamie had wanted money for food. I asked Jamie, "Why do you lie to me?" She responded, "I'm hungry," but an hour or two before that, she had told me she was at Luis' mother's, and the kitchen was free, so they were going to eat.

Anyway, I will do this. Then Jamie can earn money, and Luis. I realize you don't agree, but I did say I would help, and so I will – but only for a place to sleep and hopefully be safe. If it turns out badly, so be it, but on the outside chance that it might do some good, it's not a bad thing. I'm sorry, I couldn't just say no. If Jamie is really trying, I do want to help. You seem to think she's staying clean, and she took her tests, or so she said. We can check with her therapist to make sure. I told her, "This is only until you get a paycheck. No other excuses." I know what you're saying, but I at least have to feel that she is safe in a place for a while, and has a chance to go to work.

Love, Jerry

Hi Joan,

Just wanted to forward a few days in the life. Jamie has been doing so well, and as of yesterday, was 25 days clean…on her own. However, last night, Jerry got a page from her and her latest, Luis. It seems that things aren't working out, and she wanted Jerry to give her money to buy Luis out of the car they bought together last week. He refused, I hope, and is getting strong enough to keep saying no. Anyway, Luis told Jerry that Jamie had spent $60 to get her hair done (she is homeless, mind you) and then slipped off to have a few drinks. I don't know any more than that. Oh, yes, she is also saying that she is pregnant on top of it all.

Could we write a book?

I talked to Mom and Dad yesterday, and told them I would write to them. Please don't pass this along. I think it is all too much for them to take.

Love, Annie

Sunday, May 28, 2000

Hi Annie,

How are you? Strange you should get a call from Jamie at one. I got one from Luis around 1:45, saying, "Please call me, emergency," so I did. He said Jamie was drinking heavily. I asked if she was passed out, and he said yes. He wanted to know what to do – stay and take care of her, or walk. I told him to call a crisis center. We got disconnected. I called back, asked for Jamie. Finally, she got on and said, "Don't believe him…." He got on, she left the room, paging me from a different phone. She told me he had beaten her up, kicked her out of the car, taken her money. I told her to call the police. She said she couldn't, or she'd end up in the river, dead. I told her to call the crisis center or some shelter…do something. She said, "I need some money."

I told her she had to call these places and get professional help. She said she was afraid. I told her, "I don't have any money, so don't ask me to wire any, because I'm not going to." I said if he was bad, to get away from him. I asked if she had been drinking, and she said she had been clean for 38 days. "I don't understand," she said, and hung up. She also said, "Please don't tell Mom, and Luis told me the same thing. Don't tell Annie, she doesn't understand."

Luis told me Jamie had fallen on a broken wine bottle. Jamie tried to say Luis cut her. I tried to tell her to call the authorities, but the reason I'm telling you all this is that it happened just after you talked to her. Does that sound reasonable to you? Makes me think it might be all made up to get some money from me. At first, Luis told me she was knocked out, which would have been just after you talked. Anyway, she told me not to tell you all this, so do as you please…too much for me….

Love, Jerry

Hi Jerry,

Yikes! Of course, I believe she is hanging out with the wrong crowd, and I have no doubt that she could be MIA, but this is the choice she has made, not us. It's hard to face that fact, but what else can we do? Of course, the other side of this is that yes, it could all be a ploy to get money from you, so I say change your number and be done with it. I agree, it is all too much for me, too. Keep the faith.

Love, Annie

Hi Joan,

I have made a note in my calendar about your trip East. Let me know when you have firmed up your dates. As far as I can tell, we are around during those days. I'm hoping for a warm summer so that in between other activities, we will be hanging at the pool. I have scheduled a lot of things for the children, including time with their respective Big Brother/Big Sister – an overnight girls' camp for two weeks in July/August for Camille, a whitewater rafting weekend in June, and one week of art camp in July. Joshua's big brother will be able to increase his hours to 10 each week. He is also scheduled for the outdoor adventure series that Camille is just wrapping up. It will be for one week of day camp. He didn't want anything to do with an overnight camp. Also, mountain biking camp in July.

All of these things are paid for by a state agency, having qualified for these awesome support services through Josh's school last year. I have been working pretty closely with them during the past four months. Each of the children has a therapist from that agency with whom they meet once a week at school. Some part of this therapy will be continued throughout the summer, too.

I am continuing my own personal therapy, which has been helpful, though I am wondering if it is enough. It helps me to remain focused, but with so many things going on, it is difficult at times. What I'm finding is that nothing is constant these days. I just roll with whatever comes at me, and it only remains tumultuous. It seems that there has been no resolution to any issues:

- Jamie remains out of control. The stories recounted by her and Luis are incomprehensible. One can only believe that they have been conjured up as a ploy to extort money from either Jerry or myself, or at least a lot of sympathy. I can't quite figure it out. Her attempts at splitting are amazing. She is still living out of state – says she has a job which was supposed to start today at a restaurant, etc. She says she is 38 days clean, though Luis says she is drinking. I have to screen my calls during the day – have Chris answer when she is home, and then just flip the line over to the answering machine during dinnertime and into the night. It is most stressful.

- My son, Greg, has separated from his wife. He has admitted that his drug habits are out of control, and is trying to get help, I think. I haven't talked with him for a couple of weeks. He does not bring his problems to my table, but as you can probably imagine, I think about him and how he is destroying his life and those close to him by these actions. Cocaine, crack, alcohol – but with alcohol as his trigger. He works in the hospitality industry, and is used to serving/smelling the stuff. He told me he was getting a day job at a bank. I worry about this access to money, and if he has an out-of-control drug habit, well… Anyway, his children will be one and five years old in a couple of weeks. His ex will be moving in with her mother, about an hour south of where they are living now.

- I may have told you that my unemployment benefits have been denied until I file an appeal. That said, I have received a hearing date of June 6. It is all so complicated.

Hard for me to commit to a 40-hour work week any-where, but I obviously need the money to keep this family going. I have spent all my savings, and cashed in all my stocks. Jerry has helped out modestly, but he's on a limited budget, too. It is not easy finding a job that will pay the same salary as my previous one. My feeling, of course… and with a chip on my shoulder, too…is that they should pay to the very end. Of course, the state doesn't see it that way. I turned down a third interview because of the dis-tance from home. I have been collecting welfare benefits, which include child support due to the kids. However, be-cause the child support order was never vacated at the time I became their legal guardian, Jamie is still receiving money that is supposed to go to the kids from their father's payroll: $109 a week. This is all very complicated, and I have submitted a signed agreement to the court to get the order vacated.

• I have been diagnosed with basal joint arthritis with a bone spur in my right thumb and wrist, with the same in my left. My options are surgical repair, which has a high success rate, or try to keep it under control with anti-in-flammatory agents and glucosamine chondroitin. I will try the second route. Mom has had this, too. I saw an ortho/hand guy last month, who said he sees a lot of this in women my age, and can't figure out why…to which I replied, "Did you ever think about the fact that women do most of the administrative work and always have, not to mention motherhood, housekeeping, etc.?" This is prob-ably the least of my worries at the moment, but it is trou-blesome. The pain is excruciating – how could I work with this condition?

The house is quiet today. The children are with their dad… they go every Friday night through Sunday. Camille has her Adventure Club end-of-session program tomorrow all day and overnight, returning home Tuesday at 5. She will be hiking, canoeing, rock climbing, and hopefully having a great time. She's really looking forward to it. On Thursday, she will be going to Ellis Island on a class trip – a very long day for her last day of school.

This will pretty much bring you up to date other than to say that Chris is being as supportive as ever. We never thought our lives could be so complicated, but I am ever grateful and fortunate to have her right there. I would not be standing if it weren't for her ability to be strong, too.

Thanks for listening.

Love, Annie

"This is an incredible situation, every day a new twist. You don't need a writer for this drama." – Jerry

June 2000

Hi Jerry,

Just thought I would let you know that I got a call from an attorney this afternoon that represents Luis. He is apparently in jail, and she was calling at his request to see if I could offer any information. Fortunately, I wasn't home when she called – it came in on the answering machine. I called her back to say that I was not interested, because I did not have any firsthand information on the matter. I hope she doesn't call me again. Imagine suggesting that I could offer information. I can't. That's all for now – that's enough. Talk to you later.

(TO THE READER: *Pause if you will... take a deep breath... just as we did. And now Jamie is back and living with Mike. The undeniable chaos addiction brings not just to Jamie, but to us as well.*)

I had two calls from Jamie on Tuesday evening. The first one just as I was getting ready to leave for my NarAnon meeting. I hung up on her, and switched the phone over to the answering machine. She called again shortly thereafter and left a long, detailed, venomous message which I retrieved when I got home. Basically, she feels that because she is 68 days "clean," she should have her children back. You know and I know that it will be a long time, if ever, before she will be able to have them. She will have to follow steps and guidelines in order for a supervised visit to occur. This would be a one-hour visit with the children with both their therapists present. It would be very controlled, and Jamie would have to be following the rules totally. She would have to meet with the facilitator once a week for at least a month prior to the visit, plus have random blood draws and urine tests. She says she is clean, and this may be true of the heroin, but I don't know about the other stuff. Anyway, this would be a way to substantiate her truth on the matter. If she is able to be consistent and understand her role during an initial meeting with the children, then it is possible that a meeting could be set up in August. I am fearful that with Mike in her life, she won't be able to stay clean for very long, however.

She has been good about writing to the kids, and Mike wrote to them, also. His letter was not appropriate, and hers were borderline. She has been in compliance with keeping in touch with them pretty consistently, and that is in her favor, for sure.

At the same time, Mike says Jamie is depressed, crying all the time and cannot figure out why she can't see the children. He called to see if I would meet them for lunch with the kids, asking, "What harm would that be?" I told him the same thing: she has to work her program with her therapists. Being clean is not enough. Anyway, I found out this morning that Jamie missed her therapy appointment last week. So, back to square one, even though she is telling Mike that she is doing everything possible, and that I am keeping the kids from her. In addition, Jamie told one of my friends that she was living in her car, was 66 days clean, and that her mom and her partner were trying to take the kids away from her. No calls from Jamie directly, though I am prepared that she might call at any time, since I talked with Mike.

The kids are off with their therapists for breakfast this morning. I get a two-hour reprieve. Will talk to you later.

Love, Annie

Hi Annie,

Thanks for the update...it doesn't sound as though Jamie is living in her car, but who knows...otherwise, how does Mike know all this? I have not had any messages from her in quite a while. I guess we just keep plugging along. Life.... Oh, well, we know the road is bumpy. I'll be in touch. Take care.

Love, Jerry

"I feel her brain has been severely re-arranged, and that she may never 'come back.' This brings tremendous sadness. I think we have all been grieving for her for some time, even though she does not realize the impact she has made." – Annie, June 29, 2000

Hi Annie,

This is Jamie. I want to talk to the children. In 8 more days, it will be 5 months since I have seen my kids. I am clean...that's what you wanted, right? You don't answer your telephone or return my calls. I need some hope here. Could you at least ask the kids to write me a letter?

I need to speak to you about court dates. I have been in court six times in the last two weeks, and I have to go again this week. I need to speak to you about two things. I need answers to some questions. I think things are really out of hand. Please find the time to call me. Last time I checked, you were still my mother.

Jamie

September 2000

Dear Jerry,

The D.A.'s office called yesterday. They are the ones trying to prosecute Luis. Right now, they are trying to determine whether to try this case in county or superior court. The charge is kidnapping. They asked me if Jamie had exaggerated stories, or simply didn't tell the truth. I told them that Jamie will tell the truth – her version, of course – and that is always her reality. I told them she was handicapped in her ability to see the truth in a situation.

I can't say what to do about Jamie. She needs to accept that she is sick and in desperate need of help. She is a walking time bomb, and it is only a matter of time before she will explode.

We managed to survive birthday week, but not without a few upsets. The kids were very worried about Jamie's birthday, and the past few days have been tough, especially last night. Jamie came to the house yesterday afternoon at around 3:20 on foot, rang the doorbell, handed me a card and hat for Josh, then turned and walked back the way she had come. She looked pretty downtrodden. Dark glasses, couldn't see her eyes…very somber. It was so sad to see her walk away.

The kids and I put together a nice birthday package for her last week and put it in the mail. I hope she got it. There was a card from my mom and dad; a Number 30 toy car for her 30th birthday from Josh, plus a card with $5 in it just because he loves to receive money in his birthday cards; a silver chain with three silver rings inscribed with the words *Courage, Strength and*

Wisdom from me; and a silver bracelet and card from Camille. I enclosed a simple card wishing her all of life's best. I also enclosed a book of 10 stamps with a note asking her to write to the kids so they could be assured she was doing okay. This was a ritual Camille's therapist suggested, and it felt really good to send it off to her. Time will tell. It's so heartbreaking.

I have become a board member on our local women's crisis center. I know that I can bring experience to the table.

Love, Annie

Dear Annie,

You do sound tired in your letter. Jamie is…it's hard to describe the feelings. There is a great sense of loss. I am sure seeing her walk away was sad – I know it would be for me. I know it's hard for you.

I think it's out of our hands. She has to do something on her own and stop blaming others, get into some program…on and on, as we know. Take care.

Love, Jerry

October 2000

Dear Annie,

Thanks for the stamps. Kinda an off B-day present, but thanks. I got a card from Chris last year, but not this year. Are you still together? And Dad, too, huh? He gave me nothing. I spent my B-day alone and sad…just thought you'd like to know. But everything is getting better. I'm back at Mike's and out of my car. Why didn't you say Happy B-day to me on my 30th birthday? That really hurt. Why are you treating me so bad? When I was using, you were nice, and now that I'm clean, you hate me and keep the kids from me. You got Dad and my brother to hate me. Why? I just don't understand. Why is everyone working against me? I wish you would explain some things to me. I am not dead.

Jamie

November 2000

Hi Jerry,

I had a telephone call from Jamie last night, and a message from her today. She said she was in rehab, and that she would be released today. They want her to take methadone, **but she says she is six weeks pregnant.** Mike kicked her out – he got drunk and manhandled her, so now she is living in her car again. And so it goes. She was manic, and was talking at such a rate that I could barely keep up or understand her.

On Friday, three more calls from Jamie. She told me she had been admitted to hospital rehab unit, and would call me with a number. She asked if I would come and see her, because she didn't want our relationship to continue as it has. I thought this was cautiously encouraging. However, it is Sunday morning, and I haven't heard a word from her since Friday at around 4:00. She was to be admitted at 5.

In other news, the orientation meetings have gone very well with Casey Family Services, and we are now just waiting for the home study to begin.

This is a phenomenal gift to us, and you just wouldn't believe all the services. The financial assistance they provide to families is extensive and certainly very generous. They know how to demonstrate their appreciation for the families undertaking and committing to these tasks! I will elaborate more in another letter, but I will say that it will more than take care of us financially until the children are 23 years old!

The other fantastic thing is that they are all for family reunification and will try to make that happen at all costs. In other words, they will attempt to work with Jamie, as well. The news couldn't be any better.

Love, Annie

Hi Jerry,

Ever since Thanksgiving, Jamie has been calling me collect. Yesterday, she was at a local number. I *69'd and got her. She wanted money, said she had walking pneumonia, needed gas money. I told her no, that I couldn't do that, it was the end of the month, etc. It makes me so ashamed of her at times that she just can't understand the burden she has placed on us.

That's all from here on this gloomy day. We are going out to do a little Christmas shopping.

Love, Annie

Hi Annie,

After our last talk, Jamie did call me, and told me she had talked to you, also. She asked me for money via Western Union to get clothes she needs for work. Black pants, white shirt, something like that...it upset me very much.

I did send her $100. She got it, and called back saying she got what she needed.

She told me she would call again, but no word. If she is calling you local, and needs money and is sick again, it doesn't sound like she is working to me. So, another case of being taken advantage of.

No more news from here – I was and still am upset, as I have the feeling she was lying to me. Oh, well... I will try to send some info on Christmastime, but I don't know yet what I will do. Maybe I will try to get up sometime before Christmas.

Okay, take care – I really feel kind of sick now. I couldn't believe how upset with her I was for asking me for money. I told her last time, NO more Western Union, and of course, this time, I said, "No more, NEVER, don't ask me again."

Love, Jerry

February 2001

Hi Jerry,

Just a quick update with as much knowledge as I have at this moment. I called Jamie's work number yesterday, and as we suspected, she is no longer working there.

A supervisor said that about a week ago, Jamie was a no-show/no-call, and that she had been concerned about not seeing her since then. When I asked if she knew where Jamie was living, she said that the house where she'd had a room was now boarded up.

So, this is probably not the news we wanted to hear. If you need to reach me, I will be here, around all weekend.

Love, Annie

March 2001

Hi Annie,

Jamie came to visit, as you know. I tried to get her to stay overnight, hoping she would take it a day at a time, but no.

We talked about the baby. I said she should think about what is best for the baby and herself. We talked about some treatment plans, about her going into a place to live and get treated. She said she has her name in to the women's residential treatment program again they might have an opening in April. She acknowledged that she needs more help than we can give her. And she told me that before she got here, she was as scared as she's ever been. I hope she will do something. She really seemed fine to me, but I know she is on the edge. I told her that if my tenant moves, I will go back to the condo, and she can stay with me.

I did not give her a hard time. We went to McDonald's and had a cheeseburger, and she went on her way. I gave her $85, which should get her there with some left over. I think she knows we care about her; I think she knows we always will.

Love, Jerry

Dear Annie,

Here is a money order for $1,000 (in your name) for Jamie. Use your own judgment as to how it should be used.

Enjoyed our phone visit, as per usual, and we are looking forward to your visit in April.

Will keep you posted.

Love, Mom & Dad

Good Morning, Jerry,

I have just returned from seeing Jamie after receiving a telephone call from her earlier this morning. She needed gas and money to get her car inspected because she got pulled over yesterday and was given until 5 p.m. today for the inspection (I saw the paperwork on that.) She is pathetic, going absolutely nowhere, and I really am at my wits' end as to what to do with her. It is easy for everyone, including myself, to say no to her demands, but when we are face to face, it is far more difficult than anything I have ever done, including chemotherapy. I feel as though I am up against a brick wall with her. She is always making promises, and I know she must feel like hell because of her situation, but mentally, she cannot submit to the reality of what she needs to do. It is all so discouraging, especially when I am trying so hard with these kids.

The other day, I picked up the kids and went to the Credit Union. Just before the light, at the old shopping center, I saw Jamie standing in the parking lot talking to a friend. The kids didn't see her, and it's a good thing, because she was standing there without a coat on and you could tell she was obviously pregnant. Too many close calls.

I have not heard from her in a while, though her message indicated she would be in touch. So, I am home for the evening, and this is all I know for now. The situation is not a good one at all.

I called that women's residential program myself and talked with the person who used to do intake for new clients. She no longer handles that, but I did get some information confirmed, and that is that Jamie must have her children in order to get into the program. This is most unfortunate, because I think it was my last hope for her to have a place to go. I don't know where to send her now.

Casey Family Services can only counsel her regarding the kids, as far as I can tell. I had been optimistic about their help in other areas, but since Jamie has not been in this with them, they cannot offer her anything.

She keeps burning her bridges, and wants to do it her way. Well, her way is no way out. My therapist says to turn off the phone and the wallet, and this is the last time I will give her money. If you make another arrangement, please leave me out of it for my sanity. I don't think you understand what she does to me.

Love, Annie

"I wish I felt Jamie was clean, but I don't really feel that way, do you? I've been thinking of a way to try to take care of her, but I don't have a clue yet what I could do." – Jerry, April 8, 2001

"Up front, Jerry, Jamie has been using for the entire pregnancy…right up to present. She has remained on heroin, methadone at times, and is now again on heroin, so you can see her doctor's absolute concern for this child." – Annie, May 2, 2001

New baby, Emily (May 23, 2001):
Flying by the Seat of Our Pants

Logic need not be applied now. Joy was elusive, our best attempts to find humor often failed, all we could do was hold each other up in support. Again, take a deep breath, it was one hour at a time again and again and again.

Hi Jerry,

I have talked with Jamie once today, and once last evening. She is out of the hospital, and was very tired last night. Taking the clonidine in place of methadone makes her lethargic and groggy.

She said she had an intake interview with the Odyssey House yesterday, and the next step is to meet with someone for a personal interview. They will do that at Save Haven, since the baby will be in the hospital for some time yet. There is no waiting period to get in for pregnant and just-delivered mothers. I suppose this is good news.

I will call her tonight. She said she has an appointment to talk with that local residential program tomorrow at 10, either on the telephone or in person. She is not sure how she is going to do it. It costs her money in gas, so driving is not necessary, when they can do it on the phone.

Then I learned the real reason for her trip is to pick up jewelry that will be auctioned off on June 2 if she does not pick it up by then. My feeling is that if she continues to do it her way, it will only be a one-way trip down here, and that is not good.

Love, Annie

Hi Annie,

I am glad Jamie is seemingly committed to doing this. She will need lots of willpower and support from these people. Let's just pray that she can stick it out and get well. She has a long life ahead of her, hopefully.

My love to you when you talk to her – I haven't heard from her.

Take care.

Love, Jerry

Dear Jerry,

I met Jamie today at the hospital nursery and then drove her to Safe Haven for our meeting. Our conversation was very positive, with Jamie ready to take responsibility for the road ahead and excited/scared about going into residential treatment with Emily.

I am being brief here because I am drained from the day. It started out quite upbeat and so positive for Jamie and the direction she seemed to want for herself, but that changed with a phone call from her early this evening.

Apparently, the doctor she met with was very in her face about his reluctance to release the baby to her custody without a solid plan in place. I assume that he is working in conjunction with SRS, and it sounds like they are advocating in the best interests of the baby.

Shortly after the meeting, Jamie got the news that she could not go into the local residential women's program because of a conflict of interest. Well, as you can imagine, she was just crushed. She said she would still go to her NA meeting tonight, try to get a good night's sleep, and start over tomorrow. I just felt sad for her, knowing that in her heart, she is trying to get better.

Jerry, if you can call her tomorrow, please try to reach her at Safe Haven, and leave a message. I will keep you posted. I am hoping that my faith will work for Jamie.

Love, Annie

June 2001

Hi Jerry,

I got a bizarre phone call yesterday morning from Rosemary. I was just sitting here contemplating the day, and she really turned it upside down. She said that I should check with my daughter to ask about the activities of last weekend, implying drug use but not saying it out loud. She also said that Jamie and the baby were scheduled to be discharged at 1:00 yesterday, and that Jamie had asked if she and the baby could stay with her. I hung up from talking with her and called Jamie to ask her what was going on. She was pretty defensive, saying that she had slept over the weekend, was tired from traveling back and forth to the hospital, and that she was clean, 21 days as of yesterday.

I felt calmed by talking with her, and decided to wait a while to think things over. My thought process went like this: Should I get actively involved, or should I hang back? It was tough to be me at that point, but I am really convinced that Jamie wants to get better and is willing to try whatever it will take.

I arrived at the hospital at 11 to find her in the nursery with the baby. They are both doing well.

After Emily was fed, we went to the downtown co-op, where I rented a car seat for her. All babies have to be released in an approved seat, and the hospital had recommended that we check first with the co-op to see if they had one for us. Jamie seemed very happy that I had offered to do this for them. I just hope we can keep building on this basis of trust.

Afterward, we went out for lunch. It is really hard for Jamie to stay focused on one thing and not escalate into talking non-stop incessantly. I really think she would do well to have some medication to keep her level, which would also help her with this period before she goes into a program to receive the proper diagnostic workups. Anyway, she said she would talk with the doctors about it.

Jamie is hanging in there, and I can see that she is trying.

Love, Annie

Hi Jerry,

Jamie and I talked this morning, and she remains upbeat and positive, which is a good sign. I feel I can offer her some of the support, reassurance, and positivity she needs to surround herself with. And it is comforting to know that you have been able to "stand to the challenge" by staying with her while we figure out the next steps.

I'm encouraged that she wants to get into a program but we've heard that over and again. With few choices, and long waiting periods, I'm not sure she can hold onto that thought. Sadly, it is short sighted of these programs not to have resources to help people when they admit they are ready. The whole system is messed up, too much demand, too little supply so to speak.

I also feel it is very important for her to have a physical and psychiatric exam, and she agrees. Jamie needs to be proactive on her own behalf, which she seems to be doing. We all need to continue our vigilance in supporting her.

Love, Annie

Arrangements for Emily's discharge from the hospital were made, and their stipulations were mandated. No program, no release, very straight-forward.

In response, Jerry and his wife Judy, agreed to have Jamie and Emily live with them in Maryland until such time as an inpatient rehabilitation program could be secured for them.

Annie, July 10, 2001

"We are very fortunate that Jamie has been accepted into Cameo House in Maryland, admission date of Friday or Monday, her choice! We are thrilled, but I will save that until her feet are well planted. The program is for one year – transitional residential, treatment-oriented, etc. This is the answer we have been waiting for from the Universe, and also from Jamie."

Annie, July 17, 2001

"After much conversation and an onsite visit to Cameo House, Jamie decided that the program did not offer the structure she needed. Jamie, the baby, and Jerry are on their way to another program further north, and are due to arrive on Thursday. Admittedly, Jamie is nervous, but is now more dedicated to getting on with her life rather than letting the anxiety she is feeling right now hold her back. This is a program of long standing, and it is very structured. The commitment is for one year. This is such great news...for all of us."

Hi Annie,

I am back home now, as you know. I dropped Jamie off at the place. It is too close to a city where she said she remembered going there for drugs. Hopefully, she will do well. It's an old house, and big, of course... three stories.

The woman I met there seemed nice – and strict. I also saw a few of the people staying there. Jamie was supposed to have been able to make a call on Thursday – was that to you? Did you receive a call from her? At any rate, the 10-day restriction period will soon be over, I think, and we can visit after 30 days.

If you have any news, let me know, and I'll do the same. I am praying that this will be good. They didn't have any paper forms I could take about the place. I hope Jamie will get evaluated.

Love, Jerry

Hi Jerry,

I spoke to Jamie this morning. She is getting settled in, and seemed to be doing well. She talked about an outing the group took on Friday. I am glad she did that, as it was a way to perhaps defuse some of her nervousness.

She asked me for some cash. I do not know the policy there, and said she should probably be in touch with someone who is in charge. She said she has to make her way to meetings via buses and cabs?

Thanks again for everything you and Judy have provided to Jamie and Emily.

Love, Annie

Hi Annie,

I am glad Jamie called…and that she is doing well. I did call her on Sunday evening. She told me she couldn't talk long, and that they hadn't let her call you when I dropped her off. She never mentioned anything about the buses and cabs. I would check that out first.

I'll try to call you tomorrow and tell you what I know. The things she told you, she didn't tell me. She didn't mention money to me.

And to answer your question about taking responsibility and

supporting her, truth be told, I really enjoyed it. Jamie was totally good and really didn't cause any problems the whole time. I miss her now.

Love, Jerry

August 2001

Hi Jerry,

I just finished talking with Jamie. She sounds very, very good and positive. She says she is ready to do the work she has to do in order to have a better life. The adjustment to a different way of life has been difficult for her, and on more than one occasion, she wanted to bolt. Whatever has kept her at the center has been yet another miracle. She sounded genuine, and said that there is a letter on its way to you, some of which is negative.

She was talking about Step One...admitting that one is powerless over addiction, and that life has become unmanageable. She said, "I get it...I have had an epiphany, and I really get it."

Emily is doing really well, too, sleeping from 8 p.m. to 6 a.m. She is on a good schedule. Jamie is still nursing her. She weighs 12 pounds, and is smiling and holding her head up. Her shots are now up to date, too.

Jamie said she has been reading a daily affirmations book, and how each day seems to apply to her situation. I am so proud of her, and told her so. It sounds like we can continue to do what we have been doing, and rest easier a bit. I am thankful for that.

Love, Annie

Hi Jerry,

I talked with Jamie last night and again today. She said she sent you a message this afternoon, but didn't hear back from you. Apparently, the house empties out on weekends and there is more privacy to talk.

Anyway, she is very unhappy with this program, and it sounds pretty dreadful from what she describes…including a resident who has committed murder. I know it is not a college dorm, but still, it may not be the right place for her. I said I would talk with you about how she is feeling, and that I would call Odyssey House tomorrow to see where she is on the list.

I am disturbed by this, of course, in the context of the expectations we all have placed on her. I do want to respect how she is feeling, and told her so. I think we should try to figure out the best course of action. There are other programs. She said you agreed that if she didn't like this place, you would pick her up. I don't want to be too hasty, but do you want to take on that responsibility? I know your heart is in the right place, but that is a big one.

So, I will be in touch with you tomorrow. I don't want to talk to Jamie's counselor because she doesn't seem too professional and I don't want to have retribution paid to Jamie because of something I might say. It is too bad that evaluations have not been undertaken, because she really needs individualized mental health counseling NOW.

Oh, the ebb and flow. Is it ever going to be smooth?

Jamie is very negative, and I fear that she needs more support than she is able to get where she is. I am also hearing that she is ready to bag the whole thing and thinks she can come live with you. I told her I had heard back from Odyssey House, but she said that regardless, she is not going into any more programs. This is not realistic for her, as she needs lots of help and support.

Jamie also said you told her that you had fallen. Are you okay? I certainly hope so.

It is too much for me to constantly fear for her that Jamie is not willing to participate in her own recovery in a program. She is doomed to fail if she thinks she can make it without. I hope you can try to convince her that she needs this, and that this period of adjustment is necessary for her to get on with the work she needs to do.

Talk to you later, Annie

September 2001

Hi Annie,

First, yes, I am okay...I fell down the stairs, slipped (ow!!) in my bare feet on a wet tile floor and twisted my surgically repaired knee plus my back and elbow. Now I am just stiff, but limping. Nothing is broken.

Jamie told me the same thing you heard. I tried to convey that patience is best. She told me they will recommend some therapy this week. Other than that, she was very negative. She said she just doesn't like the place. Also told me she will not go to another place or come live with me. I realize it's hard, but I think somehow, she has to try to weather this low period. More counseling might help.

Love, Jerry

Hi Jerry,

We traveled yesterday for a visit with Jamie and Emily. The kids were very good on the way. Jamie was in a meeting, but arrived ten minutes after we did. They said their hellos and we sat in the common area for a while. The kids had birthday gifts for her. I held Emily while they were getting their hugs from Jamie. Then we went up to see her room. Everyone held it together very well, and it was, in my opinion, a positive opening to the day.

We unloaded boxes and bags of clothing for Jamie and Emily from the car, then loaded everyone in and went out to lunch. We found a restaurant down the street and enjoyed a good time. The kids were on their best behavior, and Emily fell asleep after her bottle.

We went back to the house to pick up the stroller, then headed to a local museum where we stayed there for about two hours. After that we went back to the house to say goodbye and prepare for the trip home.

Everyone became a little edgy and sad to say goodbye. The kids and I stopped at McDonald's once we were out of the city, and they settled into the ride home pretty well. By the time we got home, they were wired, and unsurprisingly so. It was a long day full of emotion.

Love, Annie

Hi Annie,

I am glad the visit went well. The kids seem like they did really well, especially for visiting there for the first time. I know Jamie envisions having the kids back, but that's a big step. She has come a long way in a short time, though. Alas, there are many more hurdles to go yet. All we can do is hope, pray, and let the next day happen. I talked to Jamie briefly tonight. It was someone else's phone time, so we didn't talk long. She seemed good and upbeat. I am, too, as I know you are.

Take care, and keep well. Hi to everyone.

Love, Jerry

October 2001

Hi Jerry,

At this point, I don't understand the words behind the message I am getting from Jamie. I hear what she is saying, but there must be a story there somewhere. Apparently, she has a meeting with the program director tomorrow because she doesn't want to stay there. I know she spoke with you, asking that you come and get her. I hope you don't. She cannot possibly understand the enormous stress she is creating for us.

I spoke with the program director, and she assures me that what Jamie is experiencing is high anxiety. I told her we'd had a few telephone calls from Jamie stating that she didn't feel safe. I didn't elaborate on the specifics. She said they are taking the necessary steps to keep her safe and exploring all avenues for her recovery, i.e., mental health counseling.

What we are experiencing from Jamie is an addict's manipulative behavior, just like before she went into treatment. The only difference is that she is not using! So, we need to continue as before to support her efforts to remain in the program and stay clean. Of course, ultimately, it is her choice to stay in the program or leave.

Love, Annie

Hi Jerry,

When the children and I arrived to visit with Jamie yesterday, after hellos and hugs, I asked her what she wanted to do for an activity after we had all said hello and come out to the car. She said she just wanted to go home.

We drove for a while, trying to find something to do. She didn't want to take the bus – too much bother with the stroller, I guess. Finally, I turned into a restaurant where we could stop for lunch. She got out of the car to have a cigarette, and told the kids to stay inside and watch the baby. She said, "Don't you want to talk to me?" Well, Jerry, then she really let me have it, and I just wanted to die. I did not want this to be happening, especially because the kids were obviously within earshot. She has no consideration for or understanding of their needs. I tried to walk away from her, but she stayed in my face. I finally shook her loose and told her she needed to stop. We then went inside for lunch. The kids were trying to hold it together, and actually did pretty well. Now, of course, in retrospect, I know this trip was a mistake.

Under the guise of feeling okay, I believe Jamie was in a high state of anxiety yesterday, going so far as to deliberately try to get herself locked out after our visit and probably thinking that I would have no choice but to bring her with us. We arrived back at the center at 5:30 and there was no one to let us in, so we waited outside. Josh said he didn't feel good, and I didn't feel so hot myself. He wanted to wait in the car, and I think he was traumatized by her behavior. Anyway, one of the counselors finally answered the door and we went inside, then back out to say goodbye. It was 5:55, and at that very moment, Jamie decided to mix up Emily's bottle. I was keeping an eye on the time because I could see what was going through her mind.

I will need some time to recover from this. It is just so heartbreaking.

Love, Annie

November 2001

Hi Jerry,

Chris and I received your card this morning. I, too, appreciate our friendship after all these years. I was thinking about your message from yesterday, and I understand that you are discouraged by Jamie's actions. You know, we can only support her efforts to the extent that is feasible for us. We cannot feel guilty about who she is with or where, and should always remember that she experiences the world through her own eyes, regardless. I get discouraged, too, and I wish things were different, but acceptance is a big part of our work. This I know to be true.

I am anxious about visiting Jamie tomorrow, and part of me wishes I were not going at all, to tell you the truth. Sometimes I just get overwhelmed. I will let you know how it goes.

Love, Annie

Hi Annie,

Hope you're okay…as you said, we didn't put Jamie into this, but it's still hard. Take care. You're doing plenty.

Love, Jerry

FLIGHT: *Just keep putting one foot in front of the other*

Addiction is a master at the helm. I can go back in time to the beginning, September, 1998, that drive with Jamie to her very first rehab. So little did I know at the time how my world was changing and with this inaugural introduction, life as I knew it to be was over.

Nevertheless, naive as I was this first time I truly believed we were on a round trip trajectory; time in rehab, lessons learned, back to reality.

As you have already read, one rehab was not the fix I had thought it would be, neither was the next, and the next, and well, you are witnessing the first hand accounting, from 1998 until 2019 yet I am getting ahead of myself.

Not much matters when you are caught, victimized?, in the cycle of addiction, really. First and foremost, yourself, teetering between "the high" and possible death. And not for consideration, that precious new baby, your now abandoned children, personal possessions; a shrinking world of impaired judgment, incompetent thinking and delusions of grandeur to name a few.

December 2001

Hi Jerry,

I heard from Jamie at around 2:30 this afternoon. She was

with her friend Kelly, and was at the drugstore waiting for a prescription for Emily. Then they were heading to Kelly's apartment for now. Jamie has a meeting with the center on Wednesday concerning allegations toward the staff – which they were instrumental in forcing her to go out into the cold when the baby was extremely ill. Emily has been in the hospital for treatment, and is doing better. As you can probably guess, Jamie left the center today. She is planning to go into a different program on January 5. Maybe sooner, though, with these new developments.

She is pretty hyper, but she is with Kelly, and feels she has made the right decision. I will let you know more when she calls me back. Always something, never dull. Talk with you later.

Love, Annie

"I know it's hard on you, and you work very hard for the kids. If I had lots of money, and money could cure anything, it would be money well spent." – Jerry

January 2002

Hi Jerry,

Our family situation here is currently very tense. Chris is unwilling to accept Jamie's re-involvement in our lives, and from where I sit, this is very serious. I am placed in the middle, and obviously do not have too many choices regarding my family. It is very discouraging when she has been so much a part of the children's lives until now, and it would be rather tragic if we were to decide to separate.

Anyway, Jamie leaves a path of destruction wherever she goes in the name of "doing the right thing." It is a mess, from my point of view. Staying at the center would have been so much better than this.

Our Christmas was pretty much ruined, at least between Chris and me. We haven't exchanged gifts.

The kids are home this weekend, adding to my stress. I wish I could get into my car and drive, and never come back.

Thanks for listening.

Love, Annie

Hi Annie,

Sorry to hear about your troubles. It is always something… though at some point, I am sure we all hoped that Jamie would be well and back in our lives. I really wish you and Chris success.

I've talked with Jamie a few times, and I am hoping she will return to Boston, but I don't think that will happen.

Love always, Jerry

Hi Jerry,

My feeling is that Jamie's life is out of control. Her boundaries and contacts from rehab are gone. I hear nothing about a new program, only that she is tired, Emily is sick, and Kelly has to work, so she can't have a car. I fear they will not be able to cope with this situation for very long.

Love, Annie

Hi Jerry,

I have just returned from a busy day. First, a trip to the Casey offices this morning to give a presentation to prospective kinship foster families, then back down the highway to grab a cheeseburger on the fly, and on down to meet up with Jamie at the storage unit. I met Jamie and Kelly at 1:30, watching Emily while they removed most of their belongings from the unit and packed them into a U-Haul.

Jamie looked very good. She has had her hair trimmed to shoulder length and frosted (she said Kelly had paid for that.) She is planning to have a psych evaluation the first of the week so she can continue her medication. Her plan is to start outpatient treatment just down the street from her place, three evenings a week from five to nine.

This is a shortened version of what could have been a pretty lengthy update, but I don't have all the details. Jamie thanked me for all I have done, and after seeing the many full totes of clean clothes, bedding, etc., she said that she had no idea how much we had been looking out for her. This was very good, and I felt it was a heartfelt statement.

Love, Annie

Hi Annie,

If you get this before you go, have a great trip. I haven't heard from Jamie at all, so I finally tried to call her, but no answer. It said the voicemail was not set up yet, but I will certainly try to convince her that her own health is most important. It is very disappointing that she does not see her way to communicate with me. I think she doesn't want to hear any sermons. We try to help her, as maybe we have seen more than she has and just wish her to be well, but she perceives it as interference.

How's Emily doing? Gee, it won't be long until she's a year old. Wow!

Love, Jerry

May 2002

Hi Jerry,

I am growing increasingly concerned with Jamie's lack of interest or initiative on her own behalf. She does not view the world as others do, and therefore does not recognize the importance of supporting her mental health in ways I think are absolutely necessary for her to make progress.

I have contacted a women's consortium in an attempt to find someone, an integral person, with whom Jamie could develop a relationship, someone who could be instrumental in helping her understand what she needs to do to improve the quality of her life. She is clean as far as I know, but behaviorally speaking, she still needs, help, structure, and a plan.

The children have spent time with her, and with the summer months ahead, I have had to put schedules in place because they cannot spend the entire summer with her, nor do they want to. She presses them to visit, and they do not want to hurt her feelings, but their lives are all about finding good balance and having many different experiences from which to learn about life. In a sense, I have to protect them from her … gently.

Last Wednesday, Jamie came up for Joshua's first baseball game of the season, and it was an absolute, abysmal disaster. Josh was nervous to begin with, and in Jamie's presence, he acted out, and was ejected from the game for throwing the bat after striking out and for not following directions. You can only imagine what that was like for each of us. Of course, when I said that I had not seen this kind of behavior from Josh for quite some time, including all of last year during Small Fry, Jamie immediately took my statement personally. Then we were off on another tangent…she wants to have the kids come live with her, to which I replied, "How do you intend to support them?"

"Oh, I'll just get a job, or there must be some organization to help me."

The next day, she showed up, and apparently she and Camille had talked – making plans without my knowledge to shop for clothes and shoes before Camille's dance on Friday. You can imagine… Jamie, Kelly, and Emily arrived here at our house at about the same time the children's father was dropping off a computer for the kids.

Finally, we convinced Jamie that it was not appropriate to start out for the mall at 7:30 p.m. when Chris had already taken Camille in search of shoes for the dance. Then Jamie said, "All I want to do is just crawl up into your lap, Mom..." Which she did.

On Friday, Jamie came to take Camille to the mall after school. It was impressive that she came through – a lot of driving for her but she did it.

On Saturday, I drove Camille to Jamie's apartment for an overnight, but when I heard they went to "forbidden" places, I asked myself, *Is this good thinking?* For Jamie to be where she has a history of using, with Camille and the baby? She must have been in the same neighborhood where she was hanging out before rehab. What if Luis saw Emily? This is very, very dangerous – for Jamie to be there – and I don't think she has a clue.

Every day feels like a crisis to me because I can't manage the family in a healthy way, especially when Jamie keeps moving her borders closer. She wants to be mothered, but I just can't fill everyone's needs, and I need to be careful about depleting myself of physical and psychic energy. She is also asking me for money, and is having difficulty getting assistance from the state.

Love, Annie

Hi Annie,

I am also wondering about Jamie being on welfare... she was always getting assistance before, and even while in rehab. Actually, I know little of this system. I do think Jamie needs to work with someone and make progress. It seems to me we are returning to past times in her actions, which is not good. It's so hard to tell just what's in her mind. Right before Christmastime, we had no inkling – not me, for sure – that she was really going to leave rehab.

Annie, you are definitely in the middle, but I think it's time (and has been time) for Jamie to act on her own behalf. Easy to say, hard to accomplish. It seems like we have started to come full circle with the outside help issue. I pray that she's still clean. Somehow, Jamie has to be the one to pull through. I know she may confide in us, and we'll have to discern what's best.

Have a good night, and take care. Let me know how things are going. I can come for a meeting if you think that's a good idea.

Love to all, Jerry

Hi Jamie,

Please don't ever say that you aren't smart enough to do or accomplish whatever it is you need to do. That is "old" thinking, and does not apply to you. You are a wonderful, beautiful person who needs to figure out how to feel good about yourself all the time.

There are many tools to help you, as evidenced by your step to join our meeting today. I know it took courage. When we face our demons, they generally aren't as bad as we thought they would be. It is hard work, but growth only happens when we face a challenge head on.

Talk with Kelly about couple's therapy. You can make it work, or figure out an amicable way to remain friends.

Love, Mom

June 2002

Hi Jamie,

I am trying to call you. I hear through the grapevine that you have to move soon. Please tell me what's going on and what your plans are. Call me tonight. I left a message on the machine. Hope all is well. Take care.

Love, Dad

July 2002

On the move once more

Hi Jerry,

There have been several local Jamie "sightings" and by all accounts, the people she chooses to associate with are quite unsavory, including a known drug dealer. Obviously, we are very concerned about her influence and impact on this family, and I think we are going to have to consider drastic measures…like maybe you should bring her to your home and get her enrolled in a supportive program.

On Monday of next week at 12 noon, I have called an emergency meeting with our team to discuss her situation and how we can best protect the kids and ourselves from her chaos. I fear for Emily and feel that she will be endangered by Jamie's behavior – especially her thinking that she can live in a camper …not to mention associating with drug dealers.

It has Chris and me very, very concerned. You saw her and witnessed her behavior, and undoubtedly feel as helpless around it as we do, but the difference is that you are very far removed.

I would welcome your attendance at the meeting. Let me know your thoughts.

Love, Annie

Hi Annie,

Yes, I am concerned, too. I'll try my best to get her a place here…even if Jamie is clean, she's not thinking too well.

Let me think some more – I'll be back in touch.

Love, Jerry

Hi Jerry,

I spoke with Jamie yesterday afternoon. At first, her only concern was that Kelly was overdrawn on her checkbook, and she asked if I could loan her some money. I said no, that I could not help her. I was up front, and said the only thing I could support her with now would be for her return to rehab to finish what she started last July. She was nearly speechless when I was talking and not interrupting me. I told her I had literature on other programs, and that even if she had to go live with you temporarily and put everything in storage that would be the only way until she can find a program that fits. Her goal needs to be good mental health so she can have her family together. I also said that I was not going to contribute band-aids anymore. She knows that you and I are on the same page.

This morning, we had a round table discussion at home that included Chris and myself, my therapist, and the kids' therapists. The purpose of this meeting was to discuss Jamie's most recent actions and the chaos that has ensued. All of these people are trying to support me in remaining strong in my convictions and insisting upon treatment for Jamie, which means she needs to find a residential program for herself and Emily.

Exactly what are you willing to do, honestly? We have got to move this situation into a positive mode before she tries to figure out something even more disastrous than a move-in with addicts or pushers. I don't believe she should live with you, but maybe you could help in that vein temporarily – at least to get her moved toward something more positive.

Let me know your thoughts.

Love, Annie

Hi Annie,

Sounds like a good meeting. I am willing to go live with Jamie if she can find a place, or I can look here. Is Jamie willing to go back into a program, so we won't need a place for too long? Or she could live with me and go to some better regular meetings, health and mental-health wise. It's so hard to communicate with her. She never calls, never answers.

Just let me know what you think. All I can think is that it would have to be for a longer period of time than she has been able to keep so far...jumping around so much, you know.

I love her dearly. She has to take this seriously and stick to a plan, and not always find an excuse to leave a situation in favor of a worse one. Oh, my. I am willing to do what I can, but it has to be a place I can comfortably live, too.

You are doing all you can. This is up to Jamie.

Love, Jerry

HI DAD,

I'M SORRY WE KEEP MISSING EACH OTHER. I AM NOT AVOIDING YOU ON PURPOSE. DO YOU WANT TO STILL LIVE TOGETHER, ME, YOU, AND EMILY? I WOULD RATHER DO THAT THAN ANOTHER PROGRAM.

IF I MAKE A COMMITMENT TO LIVE WITH YOU MAYBE I WOULD GET SOME STABILITY AND FEEL MORE AT EASE AND HAPPIER CUZ RIGHT NOW I'M NOT, AS YOU KNOW. MAYBE I SHOULD JUST COME DOWN THERE FOR A WHILE. LET ME KNOW OK?

MOM TOLD ME WHAT YOU SAID ABOUT IT AND IT MADE ME FEEL GOOD. THANK YOU, DAD. I LOVE YOU.

LOVE, JAMIE

P.S.

I NEED TO MAKE A MOVE VERY SOON. I GOT SOME COURT PAPERWORK YESTERDAY AND UNLESS WE REPLY I HAVE TO BE OUT BY THE 31ST. I REALLY JUST WANT TO MOVE AND HAVE SOME SECURITY IN MY LIFE. BAD MISTAKE MOVING IN W/ KELLY. WELL, I'LL KEEP LIVING AND LEARNING.

Hi Jamie,

Yes, we can do something, but as you know, it's going to be quieter than you're used to. I know you want to be close to the kids, so think things through. We can't just jump around. We have to make a commitment, and I hope you know what I mean by quieter.

If you can find a place there, that's fine. I'll look for something short-term, but as I said, I know it's far from the kids. We can't do all that driving all the time.

Okay, talk to you soon. Take care.

Love, Dad

"If she goes down the wrong road now, I fear it's a long way back. I know she needs more than I can give her…and it's up to her to attain it." – Jerry

Hi Jerry,

Yesterday, on our way to summer camp, Josh and I stopped

at a prearranged time to pick up Jamie at her apartment and take her out for lunch. When we got there at around 11:15, she was sitting at the computer opening emails. As we walked up the stairs, I could hear her yelling at Emily.

I must say, it was depressing. She is not doing anything for herself, and this is what I can tell you about her motivation. It is nothing, going nowhere! Smoking cigarettes now in the apartment…you can just picture the whole scene, I am sure. Anyway, we stayed for about 10 minutes. I could tell Josh was getting agitated just by being there, and wanted to get out as soon as we arrived. Jamie was surprised to hear we were going so soon and wanted to go with us, saying she hadn't realized we were leaving for camp at that very moment and thought we were leaving on Sunday. Her thinking has been severely affected, I'm afraid. She realized right after she said it that she wouldn't be able to because of Emily. Jerry, my heart just breaks every time I see her like this. She is so lost and miserable, and we cannot make her do something she doesn't even realize would help her tremendously.

This morning, after leaving Josh off at camp and spending the night in a hotel, I was on my way home and decided to stop in unannounced at Jamie's apartment. This was at 11:00 a.m. The doors were open and unlocked. I walked up the stairs, and there was a young girl I hadn't seen or heard of before talking on the telephone. She quickly hung up. I told her who I was, and asked if Jamie was home. She said no, then got up and knocked on the bedroom door. A bedraggled man came out in boxer shorts, looking severely hung over. He eyed me and asked who I was. I eyed him back, and asked who he was. When I said I was Jamie's mother, he looked at me with narrowed eyes and said he didn't believe it. He said, "Jamie and the baby are at Emily's grandmother's house. Don't you know that?"

"I don't know who you are talking about," I responded. He said he was Emily's cousin. I asked what they were doing there, and he said Jamie knew they were there. At that point, I turned and left, asking him to tell Jamie that her mother had stopped by. Can you imagine this mess?!!

I am not going to allow the children back into her house until she is in a program or out of there. I don't know what this latest thrill is, but believe me, the kids are not going to be a part of it. I suggest you send her an email and tell her to pick a program ASAP. I need to cool down, but you get my emotional state, I am sure. Let me know what you say to her.

Love, Annie

Hi Annie,

I want to let you know I read your email, and I am speechless, though I cannot say I am surprised. I'm just so bewildered right now, and need to think more. I know Jamie can do better in any circumstances – she just has to try. It's so confusing that she drags herself down all the time. She could get busy and do something, and like you said, her thinking has to be severely impaired.

I have no idea what this stuff does to you. I just know it's not good. It's so sad. I'll be in touch.

Love, Jerry

Hi Jerry,

Jamie called last night. She said the people in her apartment were from one of her meetings, and needed a place to spend the night. Apparently, Kelly knew about this. Can you imagine, just inviting anyone into your home like that? I think not, and I can't truly believe her.

She was apologetic about the way the man had spoken to me, and said it would never happen again. I told her this was just another example of the bad choices she continues to make. I also said I didn't realize she had been going to meetings. I doubt her statement about that was true.

The results of Jamie's actions are just too overwhelming for me, and I see no relief in sight. We really need to place her somewhere where she cannot be a menace to herself and the rest of the family.

Love, Annie

Hi Annie,

Thanks for the update. It doesn't sound like they were people from a meeting, as the man said he was Emily's cousin?

In any case, I can understand why Jamie and Kelly are being evicted – too much turmoil going on there. I agree that Jamie must get back into a more controlled situation. It's kind of sad to think that she could be finishing up at her old program right now and getting a fresh start.

Please tell Jamie I am in agreement with you (as if that makes a difference).

Love, Jerry

August 2002

Hi Jerry,

Jamie has now moved on with an elderly man who owns a home nearby. I don't feel good about it, as she stayed there when she was pregnant with Emily.

I am going to take a hard stance with her over this move. She will not be happy, but nothing I can say has convinced her to seek treatment. I am going to request supervised visits only with the children, and plan to distance myself totally from Jamie until she gets the help she needs.

ADDICTED: Our Strength Under the Influence

It is all too much, right now. I need to process it.

This morning, I got a call from Chris, who is away visiting her family. It seems Jamie was seen the previous evening at a known local drug house. Emily was not with them. When I heard this, my heart really sank.

I am trying my best to keep putting one foot in front of the other. At times, I have waves of fear that just overshadow any positive thoughts I might have. You know, though, whatever will be will be. Reciting the Serenity Prayer over and over again until I am able to sleep at night works!

I know we have done our level best to advise and support her, and if she chooses not to listen, all I can say is that we've tried. I am concerned about Emily, and she remains a very big question in my mind.

I know that I do not have firsthand knowledge of any of the information I have shared with you about Jamie's move, but it certainly falls into a pattern of behavior we have seen before.

Love, Annie

"Her only good choice was a year ago…and that was going into rehab. Since then, it's been downhill and picking up speed." – Jerry

Hi Jerry,

I know you are putting a lot of effort into figuring out a solution, but always remember that Jamie's choices are her own, and ultimately, she must take responsibility for them.

I never thought I would be so consumed by her activities, and I am concerned for my own health, quite frankly. I look back at the last four years, and need only glance at the size of my journals and notebooks to know that we have tried our best for her.

I do fear that Emily is not getting the stability she needs, and is being set up for an unhealthy life. This bothers me terribly. What will become of her if Jamie isn't able to raise her?

Love, Annie

"Jamie said she is really scared this time...that we don't know what it's like to walk in her shoes. I hope we never do." – Jerry

~ *Chapter 6* ~

A Present-day Perspective:

We all have a story to tell

This memoir weaves a story more encompassing than my own recollections. For years, I have been a self-appointed collector, saving emails and letters some of which you have read. As this family's historian, I have diligently gathered and saved information without purpose until now.

To say my work with NarAnon has been an extraordinary experience is understated. Hearing stories of family trauma often mirrored our family, too. NarAnon was supportive to anyone who came through the doors to our meetings. Longtime friendships based in supporting each other were established.

Friends would suggest, "you oughta write a book."

Admittedly, I enjoyed writing, sharing information and throughout the years, offered articles and real-life stories on the personal impact of addiction that were often published in our local newspapers. I began to believe, the timing is right, addiction-use and overdose death continue to soar... a book, a memoir – why not now, let's do it.

I knew perspective would add a realistic connection mirrored in these pages.

In a matter of short time, I called or spoke with individual family members, explaining to each one how I needed their help to tell our story.

The responses, though mixed, were mostly enthusiastic with an eagerness to participate.

The first one to put down her words was my mom and I have dedicated this memoir to her.

With participating family members cast in supporting roles – no one more or less significant than the other – each one wrote or spoke of their lived experiences, feelings often in raw detail; heartbreak is palpable and lingering. Every story is heartfelt and gritty. Their words were often written or said through the tears of their emotions and recollections of how they felt and what they did, or did not do well.

SARAH (1923 - 2019)

March 3, 2019

My main thought when Annie and Jerry were married was that I would have grandchildren. In saving my wedding gown, I was hoping my granddaughter, Jamie, would be married in it, but it turned out that she wasn't interested, and Grandma was too far away to be of any influence.

Both of my grandchildren were more interested in their own ways of life, of which I did not approve. They became addicted to drugs or alcohol. I let it run off my back, because there was nothing I could do about it except support Annie, who was trying her best to keep the kids on the straight and narrow, and maybe help them to get rid of their addiction. Like I said, Grandma was too far away to do anything, and Annie had all of that burden on her own shoulders to help the kids – which, unfortunately, didn't work.

Greg straightened out for a while, but Jamie seemed to have a very strong desire for heroin, and nothing anyone could do to help worked. She didn't listen and couldn't even be supported, and just went off the deep end.

When Jamie was away from her family and Annie was raising her children, it was disappointing to learn that Jamie had become pregnant with Emily. Annie and her friend Chris were there to adopt Emily so she would not be burdened by an addicted mom.

I also have disappointment in the disruption of our family tree. The Avery name will die with my children, not because I didn't have any boys, but because of the actions of my grandchildren, who had children out of wedlock and with unnamed fathers.

This is not to say that I do not love my grandchildren and great-granddaughter. I do, very much. I try my best to "go with the flow" and support Annie emotionally and financially however I can.

My husband and I worked very hard in our careers, and we were very frugal in our lifestyle. My husband, Annie's father, was an astute investor, and as a result, I am able to live very comfortably – and independently, too, I might add.

Hopefully, Annie's book will help clarify addiction in the minds of many. I think this endeavor will be a great first step to help other families living a life much like hers.

One thing I can do is to pray every day for my family, especially for Gregory and Jamie.

ANNIE

October 25, 2019

My family buckled under the weight of addiction, but I'm not letting this challenge get the best of me, now or ever. Why? Because I'm relentless in my pursuit of all things good and kind and forgiving.

I draw my strength from the concepts of home and hope in my life. For me, home is a genetic predisposition for resilience. Home is roots. Home is a daily walk down a familiar street. Home is friendships.

And hope is faith.

In my efforts to battle the effects of addiction on my family, I am as complex as the disease itself. I am made of not one component, but myriad. I possess unconventional determination, and for my family, I will never give up on healing. Never.

By the same token, anyone could be me. How? By cultivating the strength of a survivor.

In my life, I have learned that you don't always need to be defined by a college education or degree. Life's experience alone can offer a meaningful journey. At the age of nineteen, I left the safety and comfort of my small hometown to travel to California and be "on my way." One good face-to-face interview opened the door to a successful career that would span 45 years.

I have learned that standing in front of an audience can be nerve-wracking, yet even if your knees are shaking, you can still speak your truth.

I have learned that marriage and divorce don't have to mean the end of the world, and can even yield strong lifelong friendships.

I have discovered that bearing children brings the greatest joy and challenges of a lifetime.

I found that the diagnosis of ovarian cancer at age forty was not a death sentence, but a life-altering moment.

I realized that losing my corporate job of nearly 20 years only created an opportunity to devote the next 25 years to my family – perhaps my biggest reason for survivorship. With courage, you won't believe what you can do to create a sense of calm.

I learned that giving of your time to someone who can no longer read, drive, or live independently can be the greatest gift of all.

I want to be remembered by my family and friends as having an unbridled passion for life; for kindness and thoughtfulness toward others. That would mean that I have fulfilled my ultimate goal of making a difference – not only for my family, but for others I have met along the way. For it is not what we leave behind, but what we have done that matters.

CHRIS
March 31, 2019

I received a letter in October 2001 from the children's mother, Jamie. She wanted to say hello and to thank me for everything I had done for her, her two children, and her mother. She said she would never forget all the wonderful gifts I had given the three of them. She thanked me from the bottom of her heart, and said she hoped I would be able to meet her new baby, who would be born later that year. This letter was a small sign of hope that Jamie was on her way to a happy, healthy life. Little did I know that this was only a moment in her lifelong battle with addiction, and that I would have to hold on for dear life before everything began to spiral out of control.

In 2004, that little girl Jamie had hoped I would meet came to join our family of four. Not only did I meet her... I would spend the next 15 years raising her and her two older siblings. Annie and I had numerous heartfelt discussions about bringing another child into our home. I panicked at the thought of this three-year-old and what the future would hold for her if we did not bring her along. The question remained, however: How would her arrival impact us all?

Annie, on the other hand, knew what she needed to do, and that was to keep the children together as a family – yet another gift given to Jamie. And so, in October 2004, we became a family of five.

Addiction is one of those words I never would have associated with my life. Growing up in a traditional mother-father household, I considered myself pretty average, and looked forward to a life of fulfillment. I was completely naïve when the first call for help came from Annie's daughter. I really believed that she would get treatment, come pick up her children from Annie's tiny condo, and continue with her life, as we would with ours.

How wrong I was. After a year of ups and downs, Annie and I made the decision to purchase a four-bedroom house for the four of us. Life became a flurry of activity geared toward raising the kids, who seemed to have lost their mother to a horrible disease. Life was full of frustration, anger and grief. I was ill-equipped to deal with most of it, and did my best to support Annie and her two grandchildren during this unimaginable time.

I soon turned much of my anger and judgment (resentment) toward Jamie. Yet with the help of outside professionals – therapists, NAMI workshops, guidance from Casey Family Services, and the support of dedicated teachers – I began to focus more on helping our family through each day instead of having Jamie constantly on my mind. I did my best to understand what this horrible drug had done to her, robbing her of a life with her children and mother.

Annie and I were doing everything required to keep our household operating as normally as we could: getting the kids to school on time, helping with homework, taxiing them to football practice and piano lessons, and yes, even to out-of-town day school.

Never wanting to add to their stress, I did my best to keep our lives on track. I could protect them from the small roadblocks that life threw at them, but the elephant in the room was always Mom's addiction – and oh, how her lifestyle haunted us all on a daily basis.

Every day brought a new challenge because of addiction. When the kids headed back to school in the fall, they would inevitably be given a homework essay assignment with a title like "How Did You Spend Your Summer?"

A simple question, yes – but the teachers had no understanding of how this assignment could elicit uncertainty in the children over whether or not they should tell the truth. For example, should they respond, *"I visited my mom in jail this summer,"* ... or *"Yeah, it was the first time I had seen my mom in a long time."*? You can imagine the impact.

Then there were seemingly simple questions like *"Where is your mother? Why do you live with two women? Is that your mom* (referring to me)? *Why do you live with your grandmother?"*

These were questions of childlike innocence that made the kids feel vulnerable and even more uncomfortable.

My biggest struggle continued to be my attitude toward Jamie. Having been an outsider, I had the benefit emotionally of not being biologically connected to the substance user. I was free to judge, resent and cast anger at a person I hardly knew.

She was not my daughter, or the mother of my grandchildren. Because of this, my decision-making was easily done with only the kids in mind. Decisions around the entire family, however, were never easy, because of the influence of Jamie and what may or may not have been going on in her life at any given moment.

I do want to recall a truth about what family really means. During one of my first Thanksgiving eves with Annie and the children, we realized after a new bed had been delivered by a local furniture store that Grover, a beloved stuffed dog belonging to Joshua, could not be found.

Our excitement about his new bed quickly vanished with Grover's confirmed disappearance. After searching and coming up empty-handed, we finally came to the conclusion that Grover had somehow eluded discovery in the sleep sofa we had traded in, and was gone.

Annie frantically called the store owner, trying to get an answer about where we might locate the missing sofa. I decided to get in my car and drive to the furniture store. Arriving there, I noticed their back lot full of old discarded furniture. Lo and behold, I spied the sofa, hurriedly parked, and ran to the pile. As I looked closely at our old sofa, I could see a protruding lump… and prying open the cushions, I was able to set Grover free!

I quickly drove back home, where I could see Annie and her grandson sitting on the stairs. He grabbed Grover, holding him tightly before running up the stairs to his room.

In that moment, looking at Annie, I discovered the truth about family. It means never giving up on people who mean the most to you… and that little boy knew in that moment that Annie and I would never give up on him. It was a lesson he could carry with him into his life.

I liken the experience of helping to raise Annie's grandchildren to a ride on a rollercoaster. It feels like years going up, but ultimately, you come back down to the bottom.

We had times of joy and happiness. I had great pride in the kids, who fought most days to get out of bed in the morning and start each day.

I watched Camille became a mom on her own, raising a beautiful little girl; and Joshua emerge from behind the closed door of his bedroom to become a man of integrity and confidence, with purpose in life.

Emily is still in high school, adding art, music and sports to her list of achievements.

And, last but not least, Annie… the mentor, grandmother, and great-grandmother who has supported each and every family member, trying to make a positive difference in lives that continue to be overshadowed by drug addiction.

We are all hanging on for another ride up that rollercoaster. What a gift it would be for it to level off for the decades to come.

GREGORY

July 26, 2019

I remember being ten or twelve years old. Chris, the older brother of a friend of mine, used to babysit for us. We thought he was cool because he wore jeans and left his boots untied. This was the seventies, and everyone was rolling their own Canadian tobacco cigarettes, and we thought that was just super cool. His parents were always gone, and Mom was working in the city.

Back then, we were latchkey kids…we came and went. We'd come home after school and do shots from the liquor cabinet, drinking crème de menthe. When my grandparents moved away, they gave my mom this huge liquor cabinet, and it was full of liquor. Twenty or thirty bottles. We'd drink from that, but like I said, I'd already started drinking.

The first time I got stoned was behind a movie theater in our neighborhood. I remember I wanted to go to the movies because we were going to get high. My friend Chris had gotten stoned earlier that week and was riding his bike, telling us he was floating on the clouds. We thought, man, we've got to do this. In order for me to go to the movies, I had to do the dishes. I got the dollar and a quarter to go, and we smoked this Columbian Gold stuff behind the theater. One person would pay, and everyone else would go in the side. Back then, people smoked in the theater. The first time I smoked, of course, I didn't get high, but the second time, it really did feel like walking on clouds. It was really fun, but it's not an everyday thing when you're twelve or thirteen years old.

When we moved north, we had to meet new people, and there wasn't a whole lot to do. I loved where we lived before because there had always been a lot going on. Back then, you could buy an ounce of pot for $100, or a quarter for $25. I didn't do any other drugs. We drank; four of us would split a twelve-pack.

My mother remarried, then got divorced. She led a bit of the single life, so she was in and out. My sister Jamie and I were in and out. Sometimes, my mom would come home, and there would be people in the house. She'd say, "Well, it's better to be here than out driving around." She'd come home and find sand in her bed, or something silly like that. One of my friends had slept in her bed without changing the sheets. She'd find holes in the closet doors from people getting into fights and punching doors. She had these Hummel figurines. Two were broken, but I didn't even know they existed. You know, you see things, but you don't see them. We always had to make sure we cleaned up the house by Sunday, before she got home. We'd have cases of beer left in the garage, because up here, you didn't need to put them in the fridge in the wintertime.

I didn't start getting into harder drugs until college. I lived on campus. I got scholarships, and I had campus jobs. Back then, in 1987-88, tuition was $10,000. I hung out with juniors and seniors. The drinking age was eighteen, then they raised the drinking age in 1986, on July 1. I was seventeen, and I was going to turn eighteen in September. I was ripping mad that I had missed it by just a few weeks.

My hometown was different back then. There were more restaurants and grocery stores. You could buy beer anywhere. My first drink out was at The Roundhouse on Center Road. I was sixteen. They didn't card you. There were more bars then: Gillies. Simons and The Black Cat.

Our town only had two cop cars. One was always at the station, so if you saw the other one, you knew you were good. We just tried to get back home without getting pulled over. Just like now, with drugs. You know, the Heroin Highway and all that.

From college, we took a trip to Canada. There were like 40 of us. We went to Montréal, where the drinking age was eighteen or nineteen. We bounced around Montreal all weekend, not sleeping. My roommate ended up getting an eight-ball. I'd always said no to trying it, but when I finally did, it was awesome.

It was a love at first sight kind of thing. Cocaine has been my love ever since I was nineteen years old. It cost me my marriage and my children. It's taken a toll on my body. My teeth are cracked and missing.

You'd be surprised how much money comes into this little town. I've done [drugs] almost all my life, but not every single day. At one point, I was over five years clean and sober. I went years without drinking, but I'd still do drugs. I thought not drinking would help quell my drug use, but it ramped it up, actually. I'd go to bars with my friends and watch them become idiots while they drank.

When I got into doing dope, which was only for about a year, I'd use about a bundle a day. That's 10 bags (tickets or singles – cellophanes with stamps on them). They all have different names. Nowadays, if you get dope, it's brown, and there is fentanyl in it. It's in cocaine, too. It kills people. It's so much stronger now.

I don't understand how people could hear about someone overdosing and be attracted to it and want to do it. But look at people who jump off of mountains, repel off rocks, jump out of planes. You'd never leave your house if you never tried anything.

I started doing dope because I was stuck in a crack house. Stuck means you've done so many drugs, it's entirely too much for your brain and body to handle. You can't get up out of the chair, you can't even say what your own name is. Nobody's getting you out of wherever you are. They'd have to pick you up and carry you out, and most times, you have to make sure it's cool for you to leave – you know, you don't see anybody outside who would block you, as far as the authorities. And of course, there are undercovers. As much as you might want to live in that world, there's always someone battling against you. If you think about it, though, everyone's the same – one's on one side of the law, and one's on the other. The cops have to think and do just like drug dealers and criminals in order to catch them. In order to think like them, they have to become like them. It's messed up. The drug dealers have to think like the cops, too.

Having gone to jail, even for a short time, I don't want to go back – but it was pretty serene, really, getting arrested and going through that process. It was interesting. And having not gotten caught until I was fifty... I wouldn't call myself lucky, because no one says, "Oh, I'm lucky, I'm a drug addict." But I'd never gotten caught.

Having this type of addiction and going through it, you know you shouldn't do it, but your body and your mind are still telling you that you have to do it. You can't not do it. There's nothing getting in your way until you complete it, or at least get to the drug. It's crazy. It makes no sense, and it's hard for people who don't have that type of addiction to fathom why you would do that to yourself. There are people out there who are pickers, cutters, alcoholics, and drug addicts...there are all kinds of realms of addiction, and one doesn't make sense to the other. To judge someone, unless you've walked a mile in their shoes...you just can't do it.

As an addict, I see everything as black and white. I don't have a lot of gray. I'm either doing it or not doing it. A friend of mine reminded me that I said at work one day (I used to use drugs at work all the time, and I'd be out for days), "Fuck it, I'm just going to be the best crackhead I can be." And of course, we laughed. It's funny, but it's not funny. Sometimes it's tragic and sad. You think, wow, how DID I get here?

When I was in school, I never really knew what I was going to do. Some people are just focused, and have a direction even before they are born. It's in their DNA, handed down. My father went to work for Bedford Construction, and his father worked for them, too. My mom was in school, she was popular; went to college, it didn't work out, and she came home and married my dad. Jamie and I are probably more like my mother in that respect. We just go with the flow, and we didn't necessarily have direction when we were young. I never thought about what I was going to do.

My mother is much better with saving money, paying her bills, linear thinking, and going straight forward and taking care of responsibilities. My father was none of those things. He was a procrastinator and never paid his bills, left his family, and passed away relatively young.

In my time of life, everybody says, "When I was thirty, I did this, when I was forty, I did this," and so on. "This is where I've lived, this is where I've been." We were only concerned about where we were going to go have a drink and get drugs.

My sister has the best stories. We think they're funny. Anyone else who reads this probably won't think so. Especially if there's someone out there reading this who has a child going through the throes of addiction. They are costing their parents time, money, effort, heartache. Many, many tears. They may not think it's funny. Jamie and I get together and laugh and talk about it, and my mom just cries.

I can understand that. I've talked to my son – we didn't talk for four years or so, and then we started talking again. He was clean at the time, and I wasn't. "Hold on," I'd say. "I gotta go, I'm taking a call, I have to go meet somebody, I have to go do something." I'm hoping that didn't contribute to him relapsing at some point in time. I understand if he and I don't speak, or he doesn't speak to me, because that could be a trigger for him. When he was younger, I don't think he ever remembered seeing me drunk or on drugs. I was, but not that he would have known at the time. Once he knew....

When they're young, I don't think anyone should tell a kid about it, drop that on a kid just because they're mad. That's not fair to the kid.

When I got married, I remember we spent the night together, and in the morning, I had this drug setup on my nightstand: mirror, blade, straw. I went through phases of snorting it and smoking it. She knew what they were, and I think had tried it, but she didn't care for it, and she told me, "If you do [this particular drug], we can't be together."

I said, "Yeah, no problem. I quit." That was always my answer to anybody. I could just lie my way through it. It wasn't the best, but it's what most addicts do. Of course, I never quit. I just did it in the bathroom, or hid it, as so many do, and was able to. Finally, when we were three or four years into our marriage, I woke her up at like five in the morning. I had just been up three days continuously, put in three twelve-hour managerial shifts, and I was all messed up. I finally told her I had a problem. We dealt with it, and I went to meetings. I probably stayed clean for seven months. And then I got into another restaurant job, started drinking – alcohol was always the gateway, as they say. After about the third drink, you're ready to move into harder stuff. It was always coke. Dope was just something to come off of the coke.

There are like seventeen charges hanging on me at the time of this writing. I always knew that at some point, living this life, I was going to come into contact with authority. You're never ready for it when it happens, but the more you do something that's against the law, especially with the severity of the opioid crisis in this country, once it starts affecting higher-ups, families, then it starts getting dealt with. Until it affects certain individuals' homes – that flips it for the country. Junkies and drug addicts are just someone outside their front door until it's been brought inside their house. And generally, it's in front of their nose, and they don't see it.

My mom helps a lot of different families, but sometimes, you don't see what's going on in your own back yard. I'm sure this can be really upsetting...when you try to do all these things, and come to find out, every single person in your family is a drug addict. It's got nothing to do with the fault of anyone –

who could have been there, who could have done things differently. It just is what it is. Everybody's DNA is what it is.

JAMIE

February 11, 2019

Today is the day I will be mindful of my talking and interrupting. I will do it, and stop saying I will try. I wholeheartedly believe in myself. I can keep my head held high and be the woman I know I can be and make myself, my mom, my family, and my friends proud of me.

I will keep reminding myself that I am okay and a good person so I can continue on this path and a new way of life. I will stay hopeful that I will no longer need drugs to feel "normal," and learn how to like and eventually love myself in sobriety. Down the road, I'll begin to help other people get well and love themselves, too. Helping others really helps me and makes me stronger.

February 14, 2019

Oh, no, I failed again

Rehab here I come

In and out...I am lost

Good angel, bad angel

The fight no one wins

Back-and-forth confusion

Hits again, what to do?

I'm running again, the smell

That familiar smell of the street

I am complete, or so I thought

Ha – the devil lies again

Rehab, here I come
Oh, relief, I can sleep
And when I wake up
The shoes will still be on my feet
Here I go again, lost....
Confusion settles down and now
I know I don't have to
Run no more, safety has
Arrived, safe I am from
The demon I have inside....

Sitting here trying not to fear
The situation coming at me
So not fair, cuz I'm trying to be
A square, telling on anyone
I can't follow through
Oh, what to do, what to do
I'm left behind making a choice
My sanity, my freedom can't be
Compromised, no one listens
I'm sick and suffering, too
Momma Bear, I am just trying
To end this fear I have inside
I'm not trying to tell the
Secrets in me cuz it's starting
To make things be like insanity
For me, please let me be
So I can make my way

Away from all the bullshit
I don't know why these
Tears fall from deep inside

February 20, 2019

I got to call my mom, and we had the best talk. I'm so happy and lucky to have her in my life, especially since I lost my dad. Mom says she never really realized how much of a buffer he was between the two of us until he was gone. She also told me his death has hit her really hard. She wasn't expecting it to be so hard on her. Today, my mom said, "I love you" to me first. It was so awesome to have her say that to me. It felt so good to finally have a mommy today. I cherish each and every moment I get with her now.

I really need to get honest and centered. I really want this. I want to be clean for real. I've truly missed that freedom – being free from heroin.

Here I go, I'm on my way
To spread my wings and
Find my way
To Gandara is another
Stepping stone
I'm so afraid to be on my own
All of you I cherish and
Will help me find my way and
Stay cuz I know this life is
A much better way
Heroin is not the help I
Need today, just you

My friends, always know
That it helps me stay
There has to be a happier
Better way, and leave the
Past where it has to lay
Cuz over the horizon is
The new way
Cuz I know you love
Me either way!
Laughing or crying
I'm here to stay
Goodbye anxiety
I have a new way
I am chasing recovery like I chased my drugs.
Hard, fast and fierce!

CAMILLE

December 7, 2021

I was 9 years old when I came to live with grandmother, Annie Augustus Rose.

I'm 32 now. I'm the manager at a local restaurant/diner. My daughter, Molly, just turned 9.

I've worked at the diner for 13 years now. It definitely keeps me busy. It's had its ups and downs … we got through the hard part of COVID when everything shut down. I didn't think we were going to make it, but we did.

When I first went to live with my grandmother, I felt a little discarded and unimportant. I didn't really understand at that age what was going on. I think anybody would feel neglected and pushed off and unimportant given the circumstances.

Things were different for me than it was for my brother, Josh. Eventually I knew more of what was going on ... I'm a little bit older than he is and at that time he was having a lot of trouble. He was always having some behavioral issues. But I kind of figured out the gist of what was going on before he did, before anyone explained it to me. I mostly just came to terms with what the situation was.

My mom had bought another house in another town where they had their own schools ... I was in 4th grade. That was the new school year. So when we went to live with Annie and Chris, it was halfway into the school year so we could officially transfer back to our original schools.

It was really hard. I definitely felt ostracized because Annie had told my friends' parents the situation and at that point addiction wasn't anything anybody talked about. And before that in the 1990s, a lot of parents were just staying together to try to save face and so having a single mom in general in the 90s was really hard.

I didn't feel good about Annie telling my friends' parents that my mom was an addict. I was really upset about it actually. Their parents would treat me differently and also I went from living with my mom who was a single woman to living with my grandmother who was with a woman at the time. In the 90s when everyone was like, "that's gay" ...it wasn't easy. It was really difficult.

It was a different kind of difficult. I always protected my brother. We're like a year and a couple months apart, but he's my little brother. So, I felt like I had to protect him even more than I needed to protect myself. You feel like your own parent doesn't want you and you wonder what's next.

Josh and I did fight a lot because he had a lot of temper related issues, but we always knew where each other was. We had a special bond. We were very close when we were kids, but we're not close any more. I haven't spoken to him in months. We drifted apart. He and I don't see eye to eye on things as adults but once in a while … every year I call him on his birthday. But he doesn't reciprocate that at all. I try to keep the communication going.

We have a sister who is 12 years younger than us. There were times when he wasn't (nice) to her. I had to tell him, "She's our sister! I don't care that she has a different father. She's our flesh and blood." So I'm very close to Emily. She's kind of like my other kid at times.

She's 20. We are 12 years and 1 week apart and she and my daughter are 12 years and 6 months apart to the day. So they act like sisters, too.

When I went to live with my grandmother, mind you, I was 9 years old, then hit puberty and then came my teenager years. So at times, living with her was really rocky. I didn't really start to rebel badly until I was about 16/17 and then I was never home if I could help it.

I felt like Josh was becoming his own person. I used to think I needed to be around for him and when Emily was a toddler, I was around a lot. And then I felt like I needed some life experiences. I needed to hang out with my friends. I didn't want to be home and reminded of all those things. I was just very emotional about it.

At that point my mother was living in town. She was sober, but I didn't trust her to stay sober so I tried to distance myself from family functions and everything. I just didn't want to participate. I just wanted to protect myself from getting hurt all over again. My mom would go to rehab and she would be doing well and then she would relapse.

Right before I turned 12, I just had this feeling she was pregnant. I remember the guidance counselor pulling me out of class and she said, "I need to talk to you."

"Is this about my mom?"

"Yes, it is."

"Let me guess, she's either pregnant or they found her dead in a ditch."

The counselor said, "Well she's not dead."

"Then she's pregnant."

"Actually she is."

I was happy to spend time with my friends. My friends' parents always were great to me. To this day when I run into them they tell me how much they enjoyed it when I came to their house. At my friends' houses they had a mom and a dad and they made me feel like I was a part of the family. I didn't have to think of all the drama. It was nice to have a break. I didn't have to have it all in my face … I didn't have to think about it.

After high school graduation, before that, I was working. I enrolled in a local community college here but I didn't enjoy it because I wanted to do it, it was because Annie wanted me to do it. And I really always wanted to make her proud because she has had so much disappointment in her life. But I ended up dropping out. I didn't enjoy it at all. I actually tried doing online courses after Molly was born. It was around the time my great grandfather passed away. I just couldn't concentrate and I was just really messed up about it, so I just started doing really poorly. But I had been working in restaurants forever and I was working at the diner so it's kind of my niche in life, I guess, serving people.

When we were younger, when we first went to live with Annie, we would go to visit my great grandparents at least a few times a year. We would visit them in Washington, D.C. and at their home in Albuquerque. I loved visiting them… I was really close to them. And when Great Gramps passed away, I had a whole mental breakdown.

I remember when I was little they would come to my grand-mother's house. My Great Gramps would set up the barbecue in the backyard and I would help him chop the salad; he would chop everything up super super tiny. I remember his laugh … he was just the best man I ever met.

I'm really at a super sensitive time right now around Molly's birthday. This is around the time of year we went to live with Annie and I'm reminded that I was Molly's age when my mom did these things and hurt me and it scares me. I just have always tried not to do the things that hurt my brother and me. I just try to be the best mom I can be and when I had this revelation that this was the time I went to live with Annie, I just … I just don't want to be a bad mom.

I remember the good times with my mom when I was younger – like snuggling in bed and making homemade pop-corn, watching movies on rainy days and doing fun things, hav-ing adventures, one-on-one times with her. When I was little, I had a sibling. Molly is my only child so she has my undivided attention. I like to think we have a really good relationship. She's the greatest kid ever. Part of me feels like I could be a better mom, I mean we could always try to be better. I'm just afraid that … she's going to think of me the way I think of my mom in a weird way.

But I think we have a pretty good relationship. I can tell when something has happened at school as soon as I see her. I'll ask her about it and she says, "Mom promise you won't get mad."

She has such a big heart and she just wants to love everyone, if someone is having a bad day she has to cheer them up. She's just so compassionate for a 9-year-old. And sometimes kids just have bad days, kids are human, too. She'll say that someone was having a really bad day so "I was just trying to help them turn their day around but then they were mean to me again and again and again."

I just tell her, "Molly, sometimes we just have to give people their space and let them have their bad day. It's not your job to fix their day. You were trying to be a good friend to them and they weren't ready to receive it yet. So it is what it is, but I'm not mad."

Molly calls my mother Nana. My mother and I have a very rocky relationship for obvious reasons, and she wasn't allowed to see Molly for the first year of her life because of some situations that unfolded that were unfortunate. Then she was able to see her and she had her for sleepovers... actually Gram had her for her first sleepover.

But I haven't explained things to her yet because I don't know even how to start explaining it to her. Every time that Jamie has relapsed or been in rehab, I just tell her that Nana is sick and unfortunately we can't go see her right now. It's OK to be sad about it, we can write a letter to her or whatever will make Molly feel better.

There are times when Molly will ask if we can call her and I have to tell her that Nana is really sick right now and we can't talk to her. She knows she is not dying, but when my mom gets into this mental state, I can't deal with her. She will just say things or suggest things ... She'll tell Molly, "Tell your mom you want to come see your nana." And I'll say, "Don't tell my child to do things that she can't."

Jamie knows that when she's not in the right mindset or manic or doing drugs, I don't want Molly to see her like that. I have had to see her like that for years and years and I don't want that for my daughter. I'm trying to protect her while allowing her to have some kind of relationship, but it's really difficult because sometimes Jamie will be like, "Well I'm your mother and you can't talk to me like that." But I say, "No, if you're my mother then act like it. I'm a grown up woman and if I tell you to get out of my house, you get out of my house. Period. If I feel like you are not safe around my child, I will do everything to protect my child. My child comes first."

Any child who has experienced trauma like I did will re-member it, and as an adult they will not want their child to live it. I try not to put her in positions that I was put in. I just don't want her to grow up really fast like I had to. I want her to be a child for as long as she can.

Looking back, when I was a kid, there were things that I would think, oh that was weird or sketchy ... but my mom tried her best. She always pulled through for every single holiday or birthday. We always had food on the table and she worked so hard. I think I get my work ethic from her because she always worked so hard to make sure we had what we needed. There were definitely times when things really were not good and really bad, but it was like that until it got really bad.

My grandmother put me in therapy immediately. I think she was trying to pull out all this negativity immediately because Jamie really was a good mom. That's why I give her all these chances. I know she's in there somewhere ... where is she?

My sister has never seen her be a good mom so she doesn't understand why I give her chance after chance. I've told Emily that I understand she never had this version of her and I'll tell her what she was like when she was younger. She had me when she was 18 and Emily is like, "Wow she was a good mom, wasn't she."

"Yeah, she really was."

ANDREW
April 2018

I wrote this in April of 2018, though I didn't get clean until November 21 of that same year. Today, celebrating a year clean is a miracle. However, it isn't the first time I have been here. The struggle is real. I don't take credit for my life today. God gave me grace! I didn't do this – WE DID THIS. WE DO RECOVER.

I am forever grateful to those who have saved my life, one day at a time.

Dear Heroin,

You were my first love, my dearest friend, my favorite companion. The only solution I had found for the void within my spirit.

Our first encounter showed me a glimpse of the relationship we would grow to have. I put you before my girlfriend, for you became my wife. I had always kept drugs with me in secret. They were my mistress, but you were different.

Without a single thought, I would sacrifice my life for you. Blinded by my obsession, I failed to see that when you came into my life, my spirit went out.

As time went on, my infatuation with you grew. The more I paid attention to you, the less present I became in my life. By the grace of God, I managed to keep from needing you. Soon, I even got clean, swearing you and all other drugs out of my life forever.

Two years later, I decided to invite substances back into my life. Except for you…for I knew the power you had. Despite my best efforts, within a year, we met again. This time, I welcomed you with open arms. My nostrils became your home. My body began to crave you, and soon I needed you in order to function. I couldn't even get out of bed unless I had plans to come and get you.

I did my best to stay afloat, but I began to drown, swimming in my suffering without a shore in sight. My life became yours just months into this chapter of our story. I knew I had to rewrite the ending.

I got into treatment as soon as I possibly could. I had rid my body of you, but I kept you in the back of my mind. Within a month of my release, you were back in my nose, where you knew you belonged.

This time, you took everything. My financial security, every relationship I held dear to my heart…you had me all to yourself. Even with all of you, it still wasn't enough. I needed more. I needed a new way to feel you. I had sworn that I would NEVER become a junkie, yet in no time at all, that needle tore through my skin and penetrated my vein. Once I saw the blood draw back, I knew relief was on its way. As the belt released, so did the tension in my mind, body, and spirit.

Finally, the magic had returned. It was like meeting you for the first time all over again – but this time, it was love. I knew I had met the devil. At that point, you took my faith, my soul, my family, the love of my life, and the will to live…but most of all, you took my ability to live without you. I fell to my knees many times in fear that only you could stand to pick me up again, for everyone around had given up on me.

I knew I must get away from you.

I knew you would kill me. Worst of all, I knew if you didn't, I would keep living in constant pain, suffering, and isolation. Today, I have finally broken free of the constant wondering about whether or not what I was loading into that spoon would be the end of me.

Since getting clean, I've lost my insecurities, and I have surely lost the fear that for so long has kept me paralyzed from living in the moment. I now allow myself to heal. I have lost the need to isolate. I have reconnected with my spirit as well as my higher power. I have lost the desire to die, and found the willingness to live.

Goodbye, my dear enemy.

I know that without me…you will find another.

By now, I know that with us, it was just lust. I was never your lover.

All you ever did was give me a temporary solution.

With you gone, I've cleared the air. You were only pollution.

P.S. Truth be told, I wish we'd never met. But since we have, I must take off the mask so that I can help the rest.

Sincerely, Andy

A leader in the fight against you.

CASSIE

December 7, 2021

I'm 22. I just graduated from college. I live in Virginia right now but I'm about to move to Arizona – a big cross country move. I've been living here in Virginia pretty much my whole life. A lot of my coworkers live in Arizona so I'm making that move to kind of get away from here. I feel like I've seen everything there is to see and I'd like to explore something else.

I work for a PR company.

My whole family – my mom's side of the family – lives here. So I'm the first one to leave this side of the coast. Everyone is really sad and all of that jazz. So, I'll be moving at the end of the month (December 2021) and my mom will be driving with me across the country and then flying back.

I'm moving with my girlfriend…actually, she's my fiancée now.

I went to college just an hour away. I have never gone more than two hours away from my family. I've been so close to my mom growing up. I was always thinking about where I would move to when I grew up and I thought I would move to New York or Washington D.C. or somewhere really close to home. When I was younger I wanted to go really far away like Paris and then growing up I was so scared to go anywhere. Then I went to Arizona and I fell in love with it and I thought if I didn't move right now, I was never going to leave.

I always thought my sisters and brothers would be the ones to leave, but they all still live close to each other and close to home.

I have a sister and brother by blood and a step sister and step brother. I just have one brother who we share the same father. My sister and I just share my mom and she has a different dad.

My mom and dad got separated when she was still pregnant with me. So I don't think it affected me as much as it did my brother because he was about 4 and I was 1 when they divorced. He was really wrecked by it, but it bothered me to see him so upset. We were really close. For me, I just really didn't think about it. I always had my mom and I was always OK with that. So my mom was and is both my parent figures.

We would go and visit my dad annually; once in the summer and once in the winter. I thought that was totally normal. My friends all had dads at home and I thought "that's cool." But I'll go visit my dad and that was my normal.

My brother was angry. He was the only boy in the house… it was me, my sister and my mom and him. So he needed a father figure and I really didn't care about the whole thing. It really didn't register with me that my life wasn't normal until I was about 9 or 10 and my dad started appearing in my life less and less – not calling as much, not visiting as much or we would go and visit him and he was in a different house every single time I would visit. He didn't have a car, he didn't have electricity and I thought "this was weird." I knew that was not normal.

My brother was lashing out at me and lashing out at my mom. I would ask him why he was acting like that. My dad stopped sending birthday presents and stopped sending cards. I was 10 so I wondered, what the heck! I wondered "what am I doing wrong for you to behave like this?"   I didn't understand he was doing drugs. My brother was trying to get my dad to love him again. I was just fed up with it. I was 10 and I called dad and told him to never talk to me again. And my dad never talked to me again! Yeah, my dad just never talked to me again.

Now, as a 22-year-old, that is so messed up. He was the adult. It wasn't my job to fix that relationship. He was the adult, it was his job. Throughout the next decade I just watched my brother try to reach out to him and fail; he struggled and my dad just was not there for him. My dad would just continue to ruin this relationship. Sometimes they would connect and sometimes they didn't. He was just so unreachable for my brother that he just continued to mess my brother up for so long.

I'm glad that I cut my dad off because I know it would have hurt me in the same way. And then again, it just didn't affect me as much because I never lived with him and my brother did live with him. I try to tell my brother to just let it go because our dad will never be the person you want him to be or that you need him to be. It just wasn't connecting for him. Our dad will never be like what our mom is. But I don't think my brother is ever going to let it go and I'm not ever going to understand because I'm not my brother.

It was just sad watching him go through that. I couldn't relate to him in that way. My brother and I were so close and I never even thought about it from my grandmother's perspective until my brother became a drug addict and now I think about it from my mom's perspective.

When I watched my brother go through what he went through, I was about 15 when he first went through rehab and I really didn't understand how bad it was. I knew he smoked weed and whatever … me and my brother would smoke weed together and I thought this was so fun and cool… we were hanging out doing what teenagers would do and then I realized he's not doing what teenagers do … it was a lot worse for him.

I remember I wrote in my diary, when I realized what was going on, that he was going to be gone for Christmas. I wrote, "Andrew's going away tomorrow and I'm not going to have my best friend through Christmas and I don't know what to do because I won't have anyone that understands me like he understands me." But this whole time I hadn't understood him like I thought that I did.

With my mom she was just never able to give up on him no matter what happened. I gave up on my dad so quickly because he just hurt me and I never saw any remorse from him.

But with my brother, because I lived with him and I knew him my entire life, I knew he was in there somewhere. And with my mom, she knew he was in there somewhere. And I realized that's exactly how my grandmother felt toward my dad.

But I never knew my dad, so I'm not going to give him the benefit of the doubt the way that I do with my brother. I feel like it's different for my dad because I'm his kid. He should be caring about me that way, I shouldn't be the one to forge that relationship. But with my brother … that's my brother … of course I'm going to fight for him. And my mom, of course she's going to fight for her kid.

So he went to rehab the first time over Christmas when I was fifteen and after that he was sober for two years. Then he dated a girl and she was only sober for six months and they were relapsing together, which was really bad. But she's clean now and she has her baby. We love her, we're still really close to her but they're not together any more. He relapsed a couple times after that and it had gotten really bad. We sent him to rehab again a few more times. We are always there for him.

There was the one time it was really bad and he went to Minnesota to a really good rehab place, but he was so far away we couldn't really be sure what was going on. I was so close to him, a lot of times I would just have this feeling when he was relapsing and he was lying about it. Even though he was super far away, the way he was talking, I just knew something was wrong. So I texted my mom to tell her something was wrong.

She said, "No, he was in rehab in Minnesota."

And I said, "Something's wrong. You have to call the rehab place."

She found out he wasn't there. We didn't know where he was and didn't know how to contact him. I was in college at the time and I had finals going on and my mom came to visit me in college. She sat me down and told me we had to prepare for my brother to die. I just thought, OK … that sucks. I just couldn't focus at all. I went to one of my professors and I just broke down and sobbing about my brother relapsing on heroin. He passed me in both the classes I had with him because he said, "I get it. I had close friends go through stuff…" So that was really nice, I'm not sure I deserved it, but he passed me.

Thankfully my brother didn't die. We got him to come home and I remember I was on the couch with him and he was detoxing and it was horrifying.

I told him, "Dude, there's got to be some part of you still in there. You're young, you're 24 and you have to take responsibility. You have to make this decision for yourself."

My mom told him she couldn't watch him kill himself and this had to be the last time. She just couldn't watch it anymore.

And now he is three years clean.

We don't talk as much as we used to. It took me a long time to forgive him. He did a lot of things during his active addiction that made me really mad. I know that it wasn't him. I understand what addiction does to people, but it just took me a really,

really long time to recognize that he may not even realize what he did and how he hurt me by not being around. He just missed a lot in my life, like my high school graduation and a lot of stuff I went through in college.

We used to go through things together and I just felt like I got totally abandoned when he was doing that. So I went through a lot of shit in college and I didn't have him ... I felt like I didn't have anyone. I felt like our connection wasn't there for a while.

Every time he was sober he wanted to come back and be like best friends as if nothing had happened without recognizing that it wasn't the same. He wouldn't say I'm sorry or I understand I missed these things or anything ... just no acknowledgment. I've gotten over it now, but we're not as close as we used to be. I've grown up a lot so I'm not holding it over his head and I'm not resentful, but I was definitely still a little bit childish at first.

But I think he's happy for me that I'm moving away. I know that he needs to be close to home even though he had dreams of moving away. I think he's happy for me and I think he knows that I need it. I feel like we're getting closer every day now.

I'm looking forward to getting away from this place because I felt pretty suffocated by everything our family has gone through for the longest time. I adore my mom and my family, don't get me wrong, I love them. But there's a lot of memories tied up in this town specifically ... I just really want a fresh start.

I never really came to terms with Andrew's addiction. Like I said, I was really angry with him for quite a while. So my mom and I relied on each other a lot ... maybe a bit too much. There were times where she probably gave me more information than I should have had when I was 15. I definitely felt like I grew up way too early... just being exposed to things with my dad and things with my brother.

So that sucked.

There is just an intensity in my family that is in all of us…, addiction manifests in so many different ways whereas like I'm scared to do so many things … like I'm scared to drink because you can get addicted to that. My brother can't drink or do anything because it's all or nothing… we all have that mentality that it's all or nothing … you either do it 100 percent or feel like you can't do it at all. So we all have had a lot of struggles with things like anxiety or depression for most of our lives.

I don't think it really bothered me until I got older that I really didn't have a dad. I pretty much just ignored it, but now it makes me pretty angry that someone can have an entire child and not care about them and not talk to them and not think about them. I'm 22 years old and he doesn't know anything about my life. And he actively fought against my brother who just wanted to know him and wanted to love him… it's just so insane to me. It's made me not want to have children because I don't want to bring addiction into their world because I know how hard it is to fight against. I don't want to bring any of that trouble to a child… it just terrifies me.

I just really didn't deal with all of it until I was this old. I think when I was really young and I really didn't understand … even when I was talking to my dad, actually, I blamed myself… I just felt like he didn't want me… that's why he left. I think I experienced depression and anxiety before I could put a name to it… before I knew what that was. Thankfully I didn't fall into addiction later in life because of that, but I've had my own struggles apart from drug addiction and it just manifested in other ways. It just sucks that he will never care.

For me, I've been struggling for the past couple of years with an eating disorder. That's been my vice since I've been about 14. In the past two years I had to be almost hospitalized… that was basically an addiction in itself to me … or like a punishment … or something that was what I held onto and my way of not doing drugs… I don't know.

That was hard for my family, and at the same time this was happening to me, my brother was addicted to drugs. And then I would feel worse about it because my mom was dealing with my brother and dealing with me. I felt like we were just these two problem children… like we were fighting for the spot of problem child and that's why I had to move home to live with my mom recently because I couldn't handle being on my own.

So, thankfully, now I have a team of doctors and I've been doing a lot better so now I can move out and my brother is recovered so we're both doing a lot better. I guess it's like a success story now. But the fact that we have both been dealing with this for over a decade and we're both going to probably have these thoughts and stuff, because it is such an addiction, for the rest of our lives … sucks. It's something I wish we didn't have to deal with… and something that is genetic, which is another reason why I don't want to have kids.

I know I wouldn't be where I am today without my mom. I don't think Andrew would be doing as well as he is without my mom either because my mom pulled us out of where we were. I had my friends telling me "you're dying, you look like shit," and I was like … whatever, you know, shut up. And Andrew was doing drugs with his friends … and my mom was the glue the whole time … we just had our mom standing by our sides that whole time, doing whatever it took until we realized what was going on. I don't know how she did it. I don't know how she had the strength to stand by someone who was so intent on their own destruction.

I remember my mom said to me, "You have two choices: you either get better or you die. Do you want to die?"

"Well, I'm not going to tell you I want to die… I may have

wanted to in the past... but now, I don't think so... not at this moment, no."

And that is what I said to Andrew a few years ago. I told him, "If you keep going like this, you're going to die."

And at some point you just get tired of the struggle. It's just so exhausting to maintain that way of life... to keep fighting against yourself because your body is literally there to keep you alive whether you're doing drugs or whether you're doing what I was doing. So it's harder to fight against yourself than to give in to that addiction. At some point I just realized it's just not worth it to be hurting everyone around you; to be hurting yourself. I think Andrew probably realized the same thing in a different way. When you have so many people fighting for you, it really helps you through it.

You think you're so alone and you think, "I'm so evil ... I'm the worst person ever..." But you're not. It's the addiction or disorder telling you that because it wants to keep you down. But you're not and you have people in your corner always ... you just have to recognize it... and that all makes it worth it.

So there is one more thing about my life and how our family addictions may have played a role:

I am with my fiancée now. Before, I dated this man for a few years, who also had addiction in his family. He was verbally abusive and terrible for me. I didn't tell my family that he was terrible to me. I just thought it would be fine, but I really don't know why. Maybe I felt like I deserved it. I dated him throughout most of college and finally I got the guts to break up with him, but I was really scared.

He had some addiction problems but he never went to rehab... he was able to get out of it himself. So I think I was drawn to him because of what was in my family. Being with him literally reminded me of being with my dad or my brother and that was the most tumultuous relationship ever.

I broke up with him in early 2020. All my friends were so shocked when I told them what he had done. Then I finally came out. I realized I like girls. I had this best friend… we realized we were in love and we got engaged this year.

I am just so much happier. My fiancée has not been through addiction … she's so nice to me. It is so much easier to be myself and stay away from bad shit. Also, it's just so hard to hate yourself when you're so happy and you're with someone who is happy for you and encourages you. It's so much easier to not think about all the bad stuff that happened in your life when you have all these positive influences around you. It was so easy to dwell on the horrible things in my life when I was with this horrible person. And now I don't even think about it. Now I have so much ahead of me.

I never used to think about a future or really even care about it. And now there's just so much to do. So many things seemed so bleak between my problems and my brother's problems… but not anymore. When my dad finally gets out of jail, I hope he can turn things around for his sake and for my Gram's sake.

EMILY

January 3, 2022

I'm 21, living in a small town on the East Coast. I've been around the country a few times visiting different places but home is definitely still on my list of nice areas. Northern New England, that is. I've been bouncing between different jobs since I was seventeen. Decided college wasn't for me after the tremendous weight of disappointment and exhaustion high school had on me.

I'm the youngest of my siblings; Camille and Josh. Annie adopted me around three years old after Jamie gave me up to foster care because everything was too much for her to handle. I came to live with Annie, Chris, Josh and Camille. Very nice

149

house with a cute gray cat, Cuddles.

As Annie and Chris tried their best to juggle three kids, two teenagers, two adult addicts and their own personal issues, I would have to say they did a better job than most would be able to. They don't get enough thanks, I think, for what they've done. Of course everyone has bad moments, and growing up having fights with your "caretakers" is normal. It doesn't reflect who they are and what they sacrificed to give, not only me but my other siblings, too, a stable and safe environment.

I think, personally, the addiction from Jamie left me with many mental issues. For me it's the trauma. I genuinely don't remember moments as a kid or pre teen. She robbed me of a childhood and doesn't care. Yes, she might feel bad, but she doesn't know how much has changed for her children. Trauma doesn't just subconsciously protect you from the bad feelings, it's all of it – the good and the bad.

A few good memories that stick out for me would include Greg and our relationship when I was younger. I chose to spend nights over at his apartment – it was something to look forward to on the weekend. He'd pick me up, we'd get a cheese pizza, turn up the rock music and make our way up the rocky dirt roads to his little friends with orange fur. He didn't have much to give, but I never minded it. I just enjoyed our uncontrollable laughter and inside jokes; I even had a chance to practice my photography there. I think we were both doing each other a favor by being there for the other without knowing it.

Jamie and Greg have left a hole in every person who would have genuinely gone to any lengths for them and it saddens me. You might forget what someone's done to you, but you'll never forget how they made you feel. And that's exactly how I feel about Jamie. She's never sat down once to apologize or talk with me about what's happened, whether it be she's ashamed, embarrassed or doesn't care, I'm not sure. When I was younger, I would have always forgiven her because she's my mother, but since growing up, I don't hold her to that anymore. It's been too many broken promises.

I have a lot of resentment for how people treated me when I was younger because I didn't deserve that … I was a kid. I didn't deserve to be left out or forgotten. However, the only way I can see moving on from all of this is just letting it go. Sometimes it's hard because you feel like you're failing your younger self in a way, but to heal properly is to let go of the feelings holding you back first.

"Uncle" by Emily

He is Maple.
He hears a loud hum, a clang from the distant sea.
He wants a steady home, love
He is Maple.

He reaches for the light, his branches growing at unusual angles.
He enjoys the laughter of the brook.
He remembers his childhood, his sister, a dandelion all grown up.

He is Maple and he lives in the moment.

~ *Chapter 7* ~

Twelve Months of Hell:

Death, deception and lies

"Both of my children are never far from my heart, and every-thing I do is ultimately for them."

– Annie

One could say I have been conditioned through life's experiences. What does this mean you ask? Extreme patience; with less reaction and more thought to response. It has served me well, especially when reactions to unexpected events must be held in check.

Jerry and I met when I was 15, the year was 1962. From then until today, we had come full circle as lovers, as parents, and during these tumultuous days of our kid's addictions, as the best of friends, we drew closer than we had ever been before. We had to.

August 10, 2018

8:00 p.m. Hey Jerry? It's not like you to miss my text. Everything okay?

August 11, 2018

8:00 a.m. Silence. My sixth sense moved me to Google hospitals near where he lived. I dialed the first number and asked for Patient Information. I spoke his name and was immediately transferred to the ICU where a nurse confirmed, Jerry had been admitted the previous evening. Belief, disbelief.

I asked if anyone was with him, the phone was then given to his wife. Between tears, the fear in her voice was palpable as she explained what had happened the night before. Earlier, Jerry felt ill. Falling to the ground, he told her to "call 9-1-1." Those were his last words.

August 12, 2018

Death arrived on its own timetable. It was 10:20 a.m. My tears fell. I was "prepared" having spoken with his doctor the night before, that it wasn't likely he would survive another day. I telephoned Jamie, I could tell she was falling apart, crying hysterically. I wasn't able to reach Greg and didn't for some time.

March 30, 2019

Of this I was once again reminded that morning. While awaiting my car to be serviced, my phone began to ring. Although highly unusual for me to answer an unfamiliar number, I had a feeling I should, so I picked up.

"Hello," a male voice asked, "Annie?"

"Who is calling?" It was always my standard response to an unknown caller.

The man went on to identify himself as a court appointed attorney, a public defender assigned by the local court in the county where Greg and a female passenger had been arrested in the early hours of this day.

Listening calmly, I went on to say, "No, I was unaware."

What I then heard was jarring... "Charges were significant, illegal drugs packaged for intent to sell, a loaded, unlocked handgun."

As the attorney spoke, I picked up my note pad and started writing down his words.

Greg and his friend had been locked up.

Once Greg would be arraigned, he would be transported to the local county jail where he would stay until bail could be arranged...or not. Bail? BAIL?

He continued, "Are you able to afford bail?"

"Well how much are we looking at?"

Though, my first thought, wasn't about money up front. It was. Why would I want to bail him?

Ah, but speak of a mother's love that will and often does over-ride common sense.

Well, it did. I knew it was wrong, but I did it anyway. I took a lot of heat from family and friends following my decision, and from myself, too.

I consulted no one, I had no one to consult. The other part of my home-team, Jerry, was gone.

I argued with myself, Greg's as safe in jail as he has been in years, off the street, and away from the lifestyle of using and illegal activity.

BUT... After 12 days of incarceration, as conditions of his release, I caved. With bail monies applied, I was now on the hook with my personal guarantee that he would attend every required court appearance. Mother and son reunited, my 50-year-old son was remanded to my custody, and although Greg did not live in my home, he was close by.

By now, familiarity has taught us addiction knows no boundaries as it pummels and intersects with the promise of life.

My son has been caught engaging in criminal activity and ultimately will pay a price yet to be determined.

Back on his home turf, my son graduated from crack cocaine to shooting heroin.

June 4, 2019

There's an old saying: Don't put all your eggs in one basket. I was reminded of it a few days ago after a visit with Jamie. On the drive home, I was exhausted; but more importantly, I was in shock at the fact that my daughter had been lying to my face for weeks.

This is just another example of the insidious nature of addiction. For months now, Jamie has been in recovery and working hard, first in detox for seven days in January, then moving up to the next level of therapeutic care – and finally, after 30 days, transferring to a residential program, where she did very well.

The unfortunate part is that she was then entirely unprepared to assume a position in a halfway house, which is where she is right now. It is a toxic environment. She lives with 29 other women, all in varying stages of recovery – or not. She tells me the staff is unprofessional, and I believe it. I have seen it. I've been in that house, and I don't know how any sane person could live there, especially someone who is trying to recover from addiction.

It just makes me so sad. What I'm seeing now in Jamie's life is chaos, and not just as a result of her own actions. I can see by spending time with her that she is not working her program the way she is supposed to. I am not sure where she will be going after this particular program, but she has to go someplace where she can get help – real therapeutic help, not just left to her own devices to figure out her life. That is not how this is supposed to work. She will be in deep trouble if she doesn't find the right program and the right fit for her.

I am so discouraged by what I saw and witnessed, but traumatized is a better descriptor for the way I'm feeling right now. You can monitor all you want, but there is something that takes over in the brain that does not allow the person in recovery to make good choices on their own behalf. Even when they proclaim something from one side of their mouth ("This is what I want," etc.), the other side almost always says something different.

I'm still extremely shaken by my visit. More betrayal, more loss, more lying. Relapse is part of recovery. We all are aware of this phenomenon, but Jamie isn't strong enough to fight this on her own. There is a new program available, with fewer beds. The push is to get her there ASAP.

Just when you think you've got it under control, you don't. There is no coasting in addiction.

July 10, 2019

Today, I am reflecting back over the past four or five weeks of turmoil: hours, days, and weeks of incidents with Jamie that have been totally unexpected, given what we were experiencing in the context of her most recent detox, which began on January 19. At that time, we had great optimism. Jamie was demonstrating staying power, her recovery was underway, and her family could breathe deeply. She was working hard to stay substance-free and sober, and taking great pride in making good choices in the first of several recovery-supported residential programs.

With her diploma of completion in hand, she approached her next residential program with anticipation, staying the course of recovery and keeping her eyes on the prize. She received another diploma of completion after this six-week program, proving that she was ready for the next phase of her recovery: a halfway house.

However, the tumbledown began when this new program failed to provide professional support services. The toxic environment in this halfway house was too overwhelming for anyone to maintain recovery. Imagine, 30 women in varying stages of recovery under one roof!

On June 3, Jamie mailed me a note, a little card that said on the front: Thanks, your thoughtfulness meant a lot to me.

Mom,

Hi, how was your day today? I hope it's going well. I just really wanted to say thank you for everything you do. I love you so very much. I do not know what I would do without you and your calmness. Talking with you yesterday was the bomb. Super fun. I love you, Mom.

Love always,

Jamie

I received this note out of the blue – of course, it was very thoughtful – and yet I had no idea that it was going to be the end of positive communication from her, which would then come crashing down into a chasm of despair and acting out – mental health rearing its head again, and my realization of how volatile she was in the context of that program. I was caught off guard. Of course, this happens to many people who are addicted to substances, and also to the people who support them. The sense that addiction can just pop right back up when you least expect it is very common, and certainly not an unusual part of recovery, but when someone has a co-occurring disorder, then to you have two things going on. You have the ugliness of addiction, and the terror of mental illness.

Three weeks ago, my daughter left the halfway house, and once again entered the homeless cycle of her life that is so familiar to us all.

She had worked diligently in her programs, and was so proud that she was finally going to be substance-free for the first time in many years. Jamie tried to remain substance-free. She continued to go to the methadone clinic for her daily dose, and successfully made appointments with her probation officer and psychotherapist.

Jamie was given a new medication to try for her bipolar diagnosis, but simultaneously, she began to spiral into serious psychosis. I'm not a professional, so I'm just going to say that was my observation as her mom. It was clear to me that within days of ingesting this new medication, adverse effects began to take place.

I made numerous attempts to get her help, but to no avail, because she was not "presenting" as a danger to herself or others. This simply eliminated any control I could impose over the situation, despite my best efforts. She was also, at the same time, taking her daily dose of methadone, and everything together just seemed to send her off the deep end.

Another significant part of what was happening during this period of time was the reintroduction of a man, Luis, back into her life – a felon from her past who also happened to be Emily's father. At one point, years ago, Jamie told us that he had raped her. Now, all of a sudden, she was saying that he was the most important person in her life, that they had a real relationship, that he was her savior.

I believe he was a big part of what went wrong at the halfway house, and that he lured her out of the program with a false promise of a different life or a better way of living.

Jamie was arrested for disorderly conduct and violating the terms of her probation. I assume she tested positive for opioids, though I haven't been able to confirm. In order for her to be a free person, Jamie needed to complete her residential treatment program. She was under the impression that because she had completed two other programs successfully, this one was optional. Well, it wasn't. He lured her out, she started to use, and here we are again.

Jamie is now back in jail, albeit in a confused and psychotic state of mind. She was brought to court and arraigned. During this process, she requested a competency evaluation, which was granted by the sitting judge. This was scheduled, but the court-appointed psychiatrist retired the day before her appointment, unbeknownst to her probation officer, her attorney, or anyone in the district court clerk's office. With no psychiatrist on staff to evaluate my daughter, this did not take place as ordered by the judge.

The evaluation was rescheduled. This time, a psychiatrist and her attorney were ready, but once again, excuses being what they are, the clerk's office had no knowledge of this rescheduled event. Now the evaluation has been rescheduled once again. Jamie's competency evaluation will determine what happens to her next.

Today, she remains separated from the general population due to safety concerns. I feel like I don't know where to go from here. Who knows what's going to happen next? It never ends. I may die before it's over.

July 20, 2019

On this date, I did not die. Without warning, it was my mother who left us. I was heartbroken.

July 26, 2019

When Jamie left her program on June 4 after nearly six months of sobriety, I vowed to take the people involved to task. I called and asked for a meeting with the program's decision-makers, and explained all of my concerns in great detail.

The meeting went quite well. I spoke for about 45 minutes, starting at the very beginning, when I first learned about drug abuse in my family, and continuing right up to the present day, sparing no details. At the conclusion of my story, the directors asked me a few questions about why I thought this particular program had failed my daughter, which I answered easily.

When I said out loud, "Now, what are we going to do about my homeless daughter?" the program director offered Jamie a dual-diagnosis residential treatment bed on the spot. I could not have hoped for a better outcome.

After taking down information, I went along down the road to the motel where Jamie had been staying. I asked her if she trusted me. She looked puzzled. "Maybe," she said.

I explained about the meeting and the offer of a safe place to live – off the street, with therapeutic care. Her first response was, "Okay," but what followed was the exact opposite of anything I could have wished.

Many events transpired after that morning conversation. Suffice it to say, as painful as it has been, after another yes and then no from Jamie, I told her I just couldn't continue to trail along behind her destructive path.

I said, "I'm done."

She took off on foot from the motel, backpack with her only possessions on her back, walking north away from me. As I waited a few minutes in the motel parking lot, I turned off my cell phone. I passed her walking, and just kept driving toward home.

Today, I am sitting with that decision. As my therapist always says, "You must first put the oxygen mask on yourself." I have decided it is time. I've been grieving my children for more years then I can remember. Their life choices have deeply affected every family member to the core.

I knew in that moment, I couldn't depend upon Jamie to do the right thing for herself.

But I knew I had the courage to do the right thing for me. I also knew, the sun would rise, the rain would fall, and the zinnias I planted would bloom and grow to bring extraordinary joy to my heart and a smile to my face.

July 31, 2019

Camille, my granddaughter, has found her mother a detox bed in a residential treatment program. Jamie can write the sequel. Only she can tell her story.

"Today, I will trust the process of detaching with love."

– Melody Beatti

~ *Chapter 8* ~

Words from the Heart

In previous chapters, I expressed gratitude for the presence of NarAnon Family Groups in my life without which I would have long ago given up. My personal commitment to attending meetings allowed me to gain insight, not just into my own behaviors or my response to my loved one, but knowledge and understanding about the complicate facets of addiction.

I have tried my best to practice the Nar-Ann principals in all aspects of my daily life; the Serenity Prayer, (especially at bedtime), the importance of detachment (this does not mean for lack of love), and finally an understanding why it was important to put myself first.

What follows next are written words of intense testimony from parents, NarAnon attendees, and much like those comments previously written by my family members, expressed with raw emotion. The heart remembers what it would sometime prefer to forget.

A parent's declaration

We are parents and family members who have been affected by the disease of addiction. We are members of your community, living and working alongside you. We belong to many different professions. We're teachers, nurses, police officers, doctors, lawyers, and managers, to name just a few. You know us if we have been brave enough to share our problems with you. However, many of you don't know us, because we are too ashamed of our problem. We fear discrimination from you.

We brought up our children alongside your children. They attended local schools, churches, and camps. They played a variety of sports for their schools, and graduated from those schools. Some even graduated from college. Our children were friends with your children, and you welcomed them into your homes. Then, one day, something went terribly wrong. We had the misfortune to discover that our sons and daughters had become drug addicts and alcoholics. We were shocked, heartbroken, frightened, devastated, embarrassed, and numb. What did we do to cause this horrific state of affairs?

The answer is simple – we did nothing to cause this to happen.

Many of our children were brought up in loving homes with good parenting. We did not cause our children to become addicts. Sadly, they made one poor choice, but for them, it has set up a lifetime of coping with a disease that has no cure. It can be arrested, and many people in our society are living clean and sober lives. In fact, that number is estimated to be about 23 million in the U.S. Your children could so easily be our children. Your children may have tried drugs and alcohol, too, but were fortunate enough not to have a genetic tendency toward addiction.

Our addicted children spiraled quickly out of control. You did not want your children to associate with them, and they were no longer welcome in your homes. We did not even want them in our homes. Their lives – and ours – became intolerable. They lied, cheated, and stole from us as well as others. They became strangers to us. They overdosed, went to jail, to detox, to rehab, often to no avail, and not necessarily in that order. They had to reach their "bottom," whatever that may have been for them. As parents, we lived in fear of the police showing up on our doorsteps, a phone call from the hospital, or the worst news of all…that our child had died.

For many substance users, their disease may have started

with prescription pain medication. When this could no longer be prescribed legally, they bought drugs off the street. In our communities, people were willing to sell their narcotic pain medication for a few extra dollars. When this became unavailable or too expensive, our children turned to heroin. Pain medications such as morphine, Percocet®, Vicodin®, and Oxycontin® are fancy names for heroin.

Our children could be your grandchildren, brothers, sisters, nieces, nephews, and cousins. Remember, our children could so easily be yours.

We need to take a stand; burying our heads in the sand will not make it go away. We need to work together as a community and as a nation to combat this life-changing and deadly disease. The statistics in our own New England community are staggering: 85 percent of our jail inmates are there because of substance use issues. Substance users need treatment if they are ready for it. Jail is not a solution unless it comes with a specific program to help high-risk inmates – and jails like these do exist.

There is a huge stigma associated with substance use, and many of us don't want to admit the havoc it has wreaked in our homes and families. However, we need to send a strong message to local, state, and national government that we need help now. Too many lives are being lost.

The tentacles of addiction are far-reaching. Grandparents are now the primary caregivers for children born to their addicted children. Other substance users are finding it difficult to get medical help for life-threatening illnesses. Unless you "walk in our shoes," you cannot understand the seriousness of this problem.

We hope you will give our words some thought and consideration. Ask yourselves how we can join together to make our communities a better place for everyone, including those who are struggling daily with the debilitating disease of addiction. This disease affects every socioeconomic group. It does not distinguish.

The mental health of substance users (and former substance users) also needs to be addressed. Many suffer from anxiety, depression, PTSD, and more, making it difficult to be successful in future relationships, whether professional or personal. People in recovery need support, stable living accommodations, and jobs. Without these things in place, many will go back to using.

Opiate addiction is receiving more attention locally and nationally. However, heroin has become far more deadly, and fentanyl is now ubiquitous. The death toll is increasing exponentially, and we are at risk of losing a generation to this disease. The stigma still exists. Some of us have lost sons and daughters. Others have children in recovery.

In closing, we ask you to please remember one important point: When a substance user requests help, their need is immediate. They cannot be put on a waiting list, or be told insurance won't cover treatment. They simply cannot wait. It is truly a matter of life and death.

This I know to be true

I have traveled the unrelenting, winding road of interacting with my now thirty-seven-year-old son, manhandled by addiction to opioids and heroin, for the past 22 years. There is no end to the ramifications of this disease and its continued impact on his life and the lives of our family. It has damaged and severed relationships, created anxieties that are difficult to quell, and marred and stolen opportunities for success and dreams for a happy future that may never come to pass. This unforgiving disease has left us saddened, angry, discouraged, helpless, and resentful.

When I am feeling broken and disheartened, perhaps having a bad day, I turn to those who I am certain can offer me a smile, hug, and a kind word. There is a room I can enter where I will not feel intimidated or judged. It is a place to give and receive from others the support we all so desperately need so we can battle the day-to-day challenges of living with loved ones in the throes of addiction. I seek the comfort of our friends in NarAnon.

I truly feel blessed to have been so warmly welcomed into our NarAnon family meeting group. My husband and I have been attending our local meeting for the past eight years. As we were so appropriately advised to do, we keep coming back. I have found this organization to be a source of valuable information, comfort, support, and camaraderie. Having a place to go and feel safe about sharing my uncertainties, anxieties, doubts, guilt, and fears has been incredibly helpful.

I have grown emotionally as well as spiritually, learned to take care of myself, worked my recovery program to help me make changes where I can, and developed acceptance of that which I cannot change.

Active participation in our NarAnon group has given me the opportunity to develop personal, meaningful bonds and special friendships with many others who have also been faced with the challenges posed by living with loved ones suffering from addiction. It has helped me achieve a level of peace I had not experienced for a very long time.

I feel it is important to reach out and continue to pay forward to members of the group, just as I have been supported and nurtured over the years.

Reading a variety of literature and engaging in meaningful dialogue helps me to become informed; understand that addiction is not a choice, but a disease; and realize the best way to work my own recovery is similar to the path of the substance user returning to wellness. As the Serenity Prayer teaches us ... we must all live one day at a time.

A path out of darkness

There it was again: that almost imperceptible rustle as something moved across the carpet in my bedroom in the dark of night. I shot upright in bed, yelled his name, and said, "Get out, get out!" I knew it was my son creeping across the floor to reach his father's billfold on the nightstand. The theft had happened before.

This event happened about 25 years into my son's addiction, first to alcohol, then marijuana, and finally cocaine. There were numerous rehabilitation programs, always with the hope for change. Somewhere along the path, alcohol had been eliminated as a drug of choice. The cocaine dominated, sucking my son in and overpowering his choices. There was no room for family or children. No time or interest in sleeping or eating. His days and nights were consumed by finding funds for the drug.

The dollars in the billfold were not all that was stolen. A camera and a television were also taken, and bank fraud took place. House locks were picked and changed. Windows were entered and car keys taken. There were broken promises, enabling, and tears. There were confessions, fresh starts, and another slip. Material possessions were gone, but the greater loss was trust, hope, peace, and family unity. There were heartaches and children adrift. Finally, there was an event that led to incarceration.

My son was in jail, filled with regret and fear of what was to come. During five months of jail time, he heard hopelessness, endured threats, and saw suicides. The hopelessness was not his. He claimed and practiced his faith, sharing it with others who were also in jail. He prayed. He read. He wrote, and I visited.

After five months, he was released to a halfway house, and eventually reunited with a forgiving but uncertain family.

Today, my son is strong, working to build relationships.

For me, I say thank you to Al-Anon and NarAnon. It was a

relief to have the opportunity to meet with others offering their experiences of loved ones moving through addiction. Always hoping for a better day, I was not alone in the struggle.

Self-care and support

My son OD'd on July 5, 2017 at 1:43 PM. He was resuscitated with four doses of Narcan®, as well as CPR, after being thrown to the ground. Come to find out, he was deeply upset with me for helping save him, but did finally agree to go through a thorough detox and then on to a drug rehab facility. My husband and I were shell-shocked, but so thankful he was alive and seeming to want help. We thought he'd be in rehab for Vermont insurance's max of 28 days, yet it turned out that he negotiated an early graduation in a mere 16 days.

Already strung out from shock and no sleep, we panicked as to how we would accommodate and support our son while protecting ourselves. We pulled all those little tabs off support group posters at doctors' offices. We Googled locations, days, and times for nearby support groups. My husband printed every single one out and started calling around. We came across the local NarAnon group facilitator, who ended a summer break to reconvene meetings, and even offered to see us before then.

We were able to attend two meetings before picking our son up from rehab. During the first one, we were pretty dramatic (bewildered), thinking there must be answers to our fears and systems in place with which we could control and ensure his continued recovery when he got out.

We immediately learned that there is NO step-by-step process that works for everyone. There's trial and error. There's trying approaches and techniques that others have used successfully, while trying not to cling tight to the same results.

Most importantly, we found friends who get us...the situations our loved ones land us in, our feelings of hurt, despair and anger. They are not afraid of these conversations, and there is no awkwardness. This does not stop at the meetings, either. I have been known to call, text, and email my friends with support for them – and to get support from them. We also get to share triumphs and learning experiences that most people just take for granted.

Two years later, I continue to attend my weekly NarA-non group, barring sickness and snowstorms. Not because I need to – because I want to. I learn a lot, and I like to share what works for me in terms of self-care. Without self-care, I'd be lost – and coming to meetings is part of that.

My son had a good full year of sobriety using Vivitrol®, and then tapered off and relapsed on his one-year OD anniversary. Three steps forward, two steps back. Two steps forward, three back.

Life with substance-use disorder can be just that, and by my going to meetings for ME, I am much better able to mitigate how it affects me. Even in times of his sobriety, there is a place for me at the table of friends. My hope is that I can keep learning about substance-use disorder and communication while practicing an ongoing variety of self-care modalities. Perhaps I can help one other person by sharing my experiences and coping mechanisms...when they come to meetings the first few times in bewilderment.

~ *Chapter 9* ~

A Final Word:

Help yourself

"I can do it alone; but I can't do it all alone." – Anonymous

As you have read, this road traveled has taught me to live one day at a time. I now understand this siege on my family, of what would come to be known as a brain disease called substance use disorder. Initially though, "it" was a thing called crisis steeped in addiction.

Now, I have learned so much more: that it can happen to anyone without concern for the color of their skin, or how much money they have in the bank, or what they do to earn a living. Addiction cuts a swath of destruction leaving more casualties in its wake than one could ever imagine.

Historically, people fall prey to opioids at their own hand. Often though, a valid prescription for pain medication will lead to continued illegal drug use. Or, a first "fix" or "try" as a choice quickly segues into the disease of addiction.

These were precisely the circumstances why I stepped up to become an active parent for my daughter's three children more than 20 years ago. I can attest that the longstanding effects of addiction are here to stay for them, and will continue to reverberate for generations to come.

There is no "winning" in this War on Drugs. Though never cured, recovery from addiction is possible.

It will be up to us, one person at a time.

With a commitment to get involved, as citizens, we have an opportunity to make a difference and a responsibility to help keep our towns and streets safe, especially for the most vulnerable of our population – our children.

Managing this epidemic through education is the best way through. Encouraging educators in the development of early intervention, hands on programs at the elementary school level, will benefit students and parents alike.

Talk with any teacher today and they will tell you how the interruption of students' home lives translates to angry, out-of-control behaviors in the classroom.

Imagine yourself having the experience of losing your mom or dad to an overdose death. Wouldn't you would feel lost, confused and angry, too?

To gear these programs toward youngsters, early intervention helps everyone understand drug addiction, and specifically how this disease affects family members, including themselves and their siblings.

Witness these young people (our future) growing up without mom or dad, such heartbreak. A parent has suddenly disappeared from their lives as a result of addiction, incarceration, or death. How can these children figure out who they are; what is to become of them; their future hopes and dreams? They are not to blame for these tragedies, but often take on the responsibility for that which occurred within their own families.

Your local library or internet access offers a plethora of good resources for learning. Books I have read, researched and recommended overflow all the bookcases around my home. Read, read, read. Media, too, offers so much information to us than ever before.

Taking the continuous flow of illegal drugs such as heroin, fentanyl, cocaine, crack cocaine and methamphetamine off the "Heroin Highways" – the back roads and local streets – is a challenge surpassed only by pursuing and prosecuting those who manufacture and distribute their products by legal means. It remains a work in progress.

If addiction hasn't touched your family, look to alternate resources. Talk with someone who lost a loved one to this disease. It is devastating; the pain doesn't go away. They will tell you how it impacts their every waking hour. Traumatic, overwhelming, watching and waiting for a loved one, and the torment and uncertainty attached to the outcome, can violate every aspect of your being.

For friends and family members of substance users who don't know where to turn, support is available through NarAnon Family Groups – a free, locally-based fellowship for people whose lives have been affected (or are currently being affected) by someone else's addiction.

The NarAnon idea was conceived to provide new insight for those suffering right along with their addicted loved one, and to help them regain hope, sanity, peace of mind, and the ability to cope. Commitment to attending as many meetings as possible is paramount to knowledge, learning how to manage your own life despite the behaviors of those around you is the first step in understanding that you, too, can enjoy a better way of living. Check local listings for weekly meetings in your area.

Seek out information on the harmful effects of a little known condition referred to as "stigmatized" on this vulnerable population.

Webster defines stigma as "a mark of disgrace associated with a particular circumstance, quality or person."

It is no secret that society treats people with addiction differently, most of which can be best described as degrading and punishing. Truth. Unlike someone with an obvious medical condition such as a fractured arm or leg, seeing an arm in a sling or a leg with a cast, generally will elicit a compassionate response. Not so for the addict.

Addiction can lie hidden and undetected below the surface – you cannot see it. Behaviors caused by untreated addiction will label our loved ones with words like junkie, druggie and crack head that bring shame and denial upon the user. Often feelings of mistrust, anger and fear will emerge that make seeking help less likely for our addicted loved ones.

Stigma affects us all. Silence hurts everyone. Stand up to Stigma.

"Life shrinks or expands in proportion to one's courage."
– Anaïs Nin

Epilogue

The initial challenges of kinship were enormous, and at times overwhelming. As the voice of an experienced grandparent, I can assure you that the daily comings and goings of settling into life and attempting to add structure where none had previously existed was complicated enough with these young children – and they were family!

With strength of purpose and unbridled support from our "home team," we somehow persevered. We figured it out by trial and error, developed consistent routines and eventually a pattern for success ensued.

As time has passed, those once young grandchildren are now young adults with different challenges beyond the scope of my authority. From afar, I watch. It is now up to them to carry their lives forward.

On any given morning, however, as I have done long before this writing, blessed with inherent discipline (and courage), I'll just put my two feet on the floor and take a deep breath. The essential component is an open mind to face that day and likely success can be achieved – never give up – no matter how small or seemingly inconsequential.

Yet, in my experience, grandparents who are raising their grandchildren experience enormous stress due in large part to the biological nature and embedded influence of their mother, and in this case, my daughter. This could not be avoided.

My daughter Jamie did not wake up to decide on that particular day twenty-some years ago that she would become an addict. And although it happened at her own hand, I will never believe it was an intentional outcome. Yet, after that initial "try," she soon became hooked.

I reflect. Difficult at best to admit ones mistakes, searching for and discovering the courage to come to terms with one's own inadequacies. Harder, though, is to watch and live with the results of perhaps a lack of understanding as a young parent, coupled with the personality traits your child came into this world with, now being played out within the life of your child without the ability to help her as she struggled day in and day out with her addiction to heroin.

And I can say with the conviction of our family's earliest experience, the focus had to be getting her into treatment.

However, through our own evolutionary processes, we found our place. Our role was more about learning how to adjust our behavior toward our daughter than controlling hers. As anyone will tell you, you cannot force anyone against their will.

This was very true, all good attempts to encourage, cajole, and bribe Jamie toward the idea of rehab were loudly rejected. It was an exhausting and a pointless use of our energy. Another lesson learned.

Jamie's numerous early attempts to get clean were met with failure. Heartbroken watching from afar; we were helpless. Her life was unmanageable and here at home, her children missed her terribly.

I was worn out from this challenge and I believe Jamie was too.

With the help of initiating a local chapter of NarAnon Family Group, I slowly began to understand how we could best help Jamie. Words like detach with love, foreign at first, but with the commitment of attending weekly meetings, I learned about the importance of taking care of me. This served me well then and now twenty years later, this has been my inroad to managing my sanity.

As I continued to work my own program, I found solace in

helping others who eventually found their way to NarAnon.

When did change occur? You may have heard the phrase, "sick and tired of being sick and tired."

Only Jamie can tell her story. Finding sobriety is probably her greatest single achievement. The disease of addiction is never cured and can only be arrested. Despite it all, proudly, what I have witnessed over these many years is her strength of character and her tenacity for survival. I am thankful to say, she has survived herself and proudly participated in this memoir.

Although much of the writing in this memoir has been focused on Jamie and my grandchildren, little was I aware that my son Gregory was in a full blown addiction-cycle too, that his life and the lives of his wife and children were in complete disarray.

Greg was out of control with an "innocent enough" habit that began at the age of twelve, smoking modest amounts of marijuana with a schoolmate. This escalated to keg parties of beer celebrating after high school basketball games, to eventual lines of cocaine during social times after work. When the allure for more stimulation grew more intense, he found himself isolating, smoking crack cocaine that became an instant, regular habit with each day.

As his mother, should I have been more attuned? Greg and his family had lived in suburban Virginia. I rarely saw him except for rare and occasional visits when he would drive with his two children north for a summertime vacation.

Phone calls between us were few if not at all.

Jobs were plentiful in that metropolitan area. Yet, despite his constant employment, it wasn't stable. He moved from job to job with few explanations. Looking back, I wondered if this drifting behavior was triggered by the results of failed drug screens.

Now, of course, I realize his life was hidden from me. I was so immersed in the daily, rapid-fire pace happening right before my eyes at home that I honestly gave little thought to my son. It was "out of sight, out of mind." My optimistic nature would dictate "no news was good news." I was blinded and oh so wrong.

In hindsight, I was able to keep putting one foot in front of the other back in those early days was due to the strength and support from Chris.

I had the greatest respect and admiration for her and knew as soon as we started dating that I wanted to spend the rest of my life with her.

Yet my daughter continued to be in crisis, and it was soon enough that we would learn the devastating news of her heroin addiction.

Among our years together, we were able to get away to re-fresh and renew ourselves, yet the toll of addiction weighed heavily on who we were together.

We became exhausted, angry, argumentative, often times barely speaking to one another. It punched us hard in our guts.

We tried – oh how we tried. But the greater personal toll of family addiction on Chris and me, both as a couple and individually, was undeniable. Despite our strengths, we simply were unable to sustain our oneness and sadly separated after 15 remarkable years together.

As the years have passed, albeit too quickly, wounds have healed between us. It took time.

Today, Chris remains a constant resource of caring in all our lives. We will always be friends, and as I said earlier, "I knew I wanted to spend the rest of my life with her," we are still in each other's lives – the best of friends – and who could ask for more than that.

My ex-husband, Jerry, and I were longtime friends right until his sudden death in August 2018.

We had long ago worked through harsh feelings that lead up to our divorce in 1979. Out of desperation we had to put those years behind us when we had to come together as friends to try to understand why the lives of both of our children had become disrupted by substance abuse. Although he put up a good front, Jerry never could quite grasp the intense and destructive nature of addiction. Despite that, he was my greatest support, always a daily email or text.

When he didn't respond back to a nightly text on August 2018, the following morning, I felt something was terribly wrong. Without direction, I telephoned a hospital in the city where he was living. When asking for him by name, I was immediately transferred to the Intensive Care Unit where I then spoke with his nurse. I never expected the unthinkable, his untimely death the following morning.

So here we are today. I am always looking for a balance and as a family, we all continue to struggle with relationships.

Our successes, however, cannot be overlooked. It must be held in high regard as we look at ways in which to cope, always reminding ourselves, "one day at a time."

Thus, this opportunity here on Earth has defined my purpose; for it is not what we leave behind, it is what we did that really matters most.

Acknowledgments

A wooden plaque sits atop my desk that reads, "Life is a Story, Make Yours a Best Seller." All things are possible if you believe.

I learned "One Day at a Time" was a way to live my life with intention. Practicing those Nar-Anon principles in all my affairs made it possible as well as these extraordinary people who walked right alongside me on this journey.

From a young age, even from my birth, the expressions of unconditional love from my grandmother, Nana, were characteristic of her personality. By example, she taught me kindness and compassion for others. Through these many years, her passion for staying connected with friends became equally as important to me.

Thank you with much gratitude to the staff of Casey Family Services – Sarah, Glenny, Jim and Kathleen – all of whom worked tirelessly for our family, one-on-one support was integral to our success, they were there for us, always.

Creating a "Home Team" of therapists, school-based clinicians, counselors and teachers, was brilliant as it encouraged effective communication. Networking was essential. Once a month we sat around our dining room table and collaborated in real time. Chris and I could depend on their commitment, and because of their strong support, we made it through. For this, I will be eternally grateful. Thank you Kathleen, Jim, Sara Jane, Kathryn, Joan, Gail, Marianne, Megan, Vincent, Norm, David and Jennifer.

With reminders of yesterday, high school classmates embodied as youthful acquaintances back then, today, nearly 60 years later, have come full circle as treasured friends. You know who you are. Ready to lend an ear or supportive shoulder, your gifts of friendship have become more valuable with the passage of time. You are all always on my heart, with thanks.

Nar-Anon friends, you have learned from making that first step, opening the door, and then making the commitment to attend a meeting or two and then you just kept coming back. Even in your sadness, your grief, and yes, probably your doubt, too, that nothing would allow you to heal from the trauma addiction brought to you hearts and souls. Yet, you survived! I watched and listened as you learned. You healed and then reclaimed your joy to participate in life once again. My heart is full of gratitude because as you healed, I, too, followed your lead. Thank you.

I began attending Sunday church services, a familiar place of long ago where once I had been baptized as a young child. During this brief weekly respite, church offered beautiful music, hymns and joy-filled warmth from the congregation. My spiritual house remains in good order with thanks in particular, to our associate priest, Duncan, with whom I enjoyed countless conversations, each one bringing comfort and peace to my day.

For Cathryn, in the midst of "Twelve Months of Hell," we found each other. Your literary background was instrumental as you reinforced my desire to run with the idea of storytelling. As you encouraged me in the early days of this endeavor, with heartfelt thanks, I hope you know how much I appreciated you.

Debra is at the top of my friend list. We were introduced in 1982 and out of necessity, shared office space for a long enough period of time. We each have our own versions of that experience, yet today, we remain best friends. Thank you always for your honesty and individuality; you are unique, you are one of a kind and I love you!

To my long-time younger friend and fellow Capricorn,

Sandy, deepest thanks... for that long weekend getaway and for-tuitous "by chance" conversations now about to come full circle. Your referral to Cindy has made all the difference.

For Cindy Casey, your talent as an editor made this memoir possible. From our first conversation, we connected. Your enthu-siasm for my rough draft was beyond encouraging. I knew right away you were the person who would believe in me as an author. With your experience and guidance, we became a great team. I will be forever grateful to you not only for appreciating my ideas, but for recognizing the importance of telling our story today. Thank you.

For Chris, with love. Your impact on my life – on all our lives – cannot be measured.

Recalling that famous Robert Frost poem, "The Road Not Taken," I decided on this excerpt as it well-represented who we were together all those years.

> *"... And both that morning equally lay*
> *In leaves no step had trodden black*
> *Oh, I kept the first for another day!*
> *Yet knowing how way leads to way*
> *I doubted if I should ever come back.*
> *I shall be telling this with a sigh*
> *Somewhere ages and ages hence*
> *Two roads diverged in a wood and I,*
> *(We) took the one less traveled by*
> *And that has made all the difference."*

Like family: Wendi and Alison, both of you successful, vi-brant women with families of your own. I have known you from your early high school days as a constant presence in and out of our home as friends of Greg and Jamie. Wendi, you became a welcomed family member for a while until graduation. As it was back then, it is so today, we are bound in friendship and love and I thank you both for being in my life.

To my family: Thank you each one who has agreed to tell your story, bearing your hearts, your truth so that others can learn through your eyes. Offer solace to just one reader who will identify with you and we will have achieved the singular goal of this memoir. If ever there was a question, I love you with all my being.

About the Author

I welcomed motherhood in 1968. That title birthed this memoir.

Due to the personal nature of our story, I am writing under a pen name to protect family members who are all so important to me. No matter how you interpret our journey, be assured, I love my family still and I still love my life here on Earth.

Life's experiences can offer a meaningful journey. What you have read was life happening in real time, family members struggling, often just to survive.

As a mother, I was shaken to the core by this unknown assailant. Yet, I did not sit still. I quickly dove in to learn more and more about this debilitating family disease called addiction. Through education, I now know that addiction is a disease, but understanding its effects, as it faced me down, has been a life-long process.

For historical purposes, let's go way back. Family roots run deep in my family, for it is written that we are descended from the first child, Peregrine White, born in the cabin of the Mayflower as she lay in anchorage at Cape Cod Harbor, Massachusetts, 1620. Proud could describe my heritage. And now, fast forward to 1998 and the announcement by my daughter that she was addicted to heroin, an addict; I would struggle to hold on to that pride.

What follows are snapshots of who I am. High school graduate, former junior college student, wife. I was barely 18.

Time and again, I've referred to crossroads and right place/right time that can best describe my opportunities in the world of business. In the early years before children, I found employment as a medical secretary. Back then my high school diploma and cheerful attitude was enough to get hired. I have often said this was my dream job.

Then children came along and I became a stay-at-home mom. With divorce, I re-entered the workplace and another administrative medical career literally fell right in my lap – one that would bring enormous satisfaction.

Remarriage, I was then back home and was hired to a position that I held for nearly twenty years as an executive assistant providing support in a fast-paced corporate environment in the natural foods industry.

A cancer diagnosis at age 40 was indeed shocking, yet armed with an experienced medical team and my positive mindset, I survived. Viewed not as a death sentence but a life-altering moment, this event set the tone, "I can do this with confidence," as I forged ahead regaining my strength and resilience.

Our family's association with Casey Family Services provided me with expansive opportunities. I participated in early childhood-related workshops and trainings. I attended conferences with guest speakers of prominence in the field of child development, including attachment-related behaviors that only furthered my ability to provide a better understanding and care needed for my grandchildren.

The value of belonging to support groups was essential for maintaining my steady balance. When I found an absence of support for families like mine, I did my research on California-based Nar-Anon Family Group and started a chapter in my hometown where meetings continue to be held today.

Recognizing the importance of support, I also participated in a local kinship support group where I met other grandparents who were in the midst of raising their kid's children, too. We used to say we were members of a club not necessarily by choice but then eventually bound by our common interests and commitment to our grandchildren.

I developed my writing skills to foster public awareness by submitting articles to my hometown newspaper on subjects such as the long-term effect of addictive behaviors on families and the value of belonging to a support group, of which I had first-hand knowledge.

Putting my experience to good use with a need to pay-it-forward to my community, activism has been important to me. I have participated in local grassroots projects always with a focus on support for families of those affected by addiction.

I was invited to become a member of a local Consumer Advisory Council and on one occasion, I traveled with community professionals to Atlanta where I attended a three-day conference on prescription drug abuse. And more recently, unexpected rewards came from providing storyteller support for not one, but two, people in long-term recovery at an event called, "A Beautiful Journey."

Standing in front of an audience is still especially nerve-wracking for me. Yet, I will do it even if my knees are shaking, because the need to speak the truth overrides my fear every time. I delivered a simple message for each invitation: everyone must be informed for addiction is a disease and must be treated as such.

As an office administrator, little did I know I was "in training" preparing for the role of a lifetime. With skills learned on the job – effective communication, planning, organizing and negotiating – you could say I was ready for the challenge.

There is no more important role in the universe than that of a mother. To be remembered by my family and friends for having a passion for life, for kindness and thoughtfulness to others, I will have fulfilled my goal to make a difference by my footsteps, not only for my family and friends, but for others I have met along the way.

Remember this: It is not what you leave behind, it is what you did that will be everlasting.